·Summer of '98·

Also by Mike Lupica

NONFICTION

Reggie (with Reggie Jackson)

Parcells: The Biggest Giant of Them All
(with Bill Parcells)

Wait Till Next Year (with William Goldman)

Shooting From the Lip

*Mad as Hell: How Sports Got Away from
the Fans—and How We Get It Back*

The Fred Book (with Fred Imus)

FICTION

Dead Air

Extra Credits

Limited Partner

Jump

· Summer of '98 ·

WHEN HOMERS FLEW, RECORDS FELL, AND BASEBALL RECLAIMED AMERICA

Mike Lupica

CB

CONTEMPORARY BOOKS

2752741

Library of Congress Cataloging-in-Publication Data

Lupica, Mike.
    Summer of '98 : when homers flew, records fell, and baseball reclaimed
America / Mike Lupica.
       p.   cm.
    ISBN 0-8092-2444-5
     1. Baseball—United States.   2. Baseball—Records—United States.
3. National League of Professional Baseball Clubs.   4. American League
of Professional Baseball Clubs.   I. Title.   II. Title: Summer of 1998.
GV863.A1L86   1999
796.357'0973'09049—dc21   98-50425
                                               CIP

This edition is reprinted by arrangement with G. P. Putnam Sons, a member of
Penguin Putnam, Inc.

Cover design © 1999 Walter Harper
Front-cover photograph © Stephen Green/*Sports Illustrated*
Interior design by Amanda Dewey

This edition first published by Contemporary Books
A division of NTC/Contemporary Publishing Group, Inc.
4255 West Touhy Avenue, Lincolnwood (Chicago), Illinois 60712-1975 U.S.A.
Printed in the United States of America
International Standard Book Number: 0-8092-2444-5
00 01 02 03 04 05 ML 19 18 17 16 15 14 13 12 11 10 9 8 7 6 5 4 3 2 1

One night in the summer, a night when both Mark McGwire and Sammy Sosa had homered, Pete Hamill called up late, the way he often does, and we talked about baseball a little more. If I came to this summer from 1961, Hamill came to it from '47, from Brooklyn, from watching Jackie Robinson break in with the Dodgers, changing Brooklyn and baseball and America, all for the better.

He was eleven the season Robinson was a rookie. On this night I mentioned to Pete that my Christopher was about to turn eleven, how baseball and the home runs had turned his life upside down, had done that to the whole house; how all my sons had come to baseball in this one summer the way I had in '61, with my father.

Pete—a writing hero long before he came a friend—said, "Write a book about that. Start tonight."

I have tried to write that book.

I could not have done it without Jeremy Schaap. Every Sunday on ESPN's *The Sports Reporters* I have the great good fortune to sit to the left of his father, Dick. I have been just as lucky on my last two books to have Jeremy as my right hand. He covered the end of the McGwire–Sosa duel for ESPN, and did so brilliantly, with a feel for the pictures, and the words of a gifted writer; he was right there when I couldn't be. He is one of the most talented young people to come into the business in years. I have benefited from his talent, and his energy, and his generosity.

Esther Newberg of ICM is a great agent; everybody in the business knows that. She is also the most loyal person I know. So thanks again to her, and to Neil Nyren, my editor at Penguin Putnam. He is class, judgment, honesty, taste: the whole package.

I received valuable contributions from three other trusted friends: Barry Werner, my sports editor at the New York *Daily News;* Barry Stanton, who writes one of the smartest and most underrated columns in the country for the Gannett papers in the New York area; and Bob Klapisch, the fine baseball columnist for the *Bergen* (New Jersey) *Record.* And three new friends at ESPN: producers Dan Weinberg, Rob Farris, Marc Weiner.

The great William Goldman is always there for me, in whatever I do.

The Elias Sports Bureau remains the single best natural resource in the business. Somehow everybody there treats me like a member of the family, and I am grateful.

I could not write a book about my love of baseball without mentioning two uncles, Tony DiVeronica and Sam Lupica, who always had time to watch the games with me, and who never tired of answering questions about Joe DiMaggio.

And once more, these two women: my mother, Lee Lupica, who has always been the quiet champion of our family, always had enough love and strength for everyone, over all the seasons of my life; and my wife, Taylor.

The first time Jets coach Bill Parcells met Taylor McKelvy Lupica, he called me up the next day and said, "You overmarried." I already knew. It is a happy world I describe for our family in this book: My amazing wife is the one who has done the most to create it for all of us. We now have our beautiful Hannah, born a month after the World Series ended, on DiMaggio's 84th birthday, as it turned out. When she is old enough, I will write her a note in the night, like the notes I wrote for my sons during the summer of '98, and it will contain the best possible advice:

Watch every move your mother makes.

I have also made her mother this promise: I won't buy Hannah her first baseball glove for a while.

Not until she is three, anyway.

For Bene and Lee.
For Taylor and the boys.
And for Hannah.

• *contents* •

·Summer of '98·

March

ALEX, MY SEVEN-YEAR-OLD, HAD THE MARK MCGWIRE card I'd bought him in the souvenir shop, holding on to it like it was a winning lottery ticket.

Or maybe just a ticket to the whole season, the first that would ever really matter to him, the one that would make him care.

The season starting right now for him, spring training on a Sunday afternoon, McGwire right there in front of him.

The McGwire card was in a plastic case, made to look like a miniature plaque. Alex liked the looks of that. He is the keeper of things in the house. Of my three sons, he is the nester. Next to his bed, on the floor, he lays out autographed balls and bats and caps and trophies and signed photographs and what he calls his "special cards." The walls are now covered with posters of his favorite players, color photographs he has ripped from the sports magazines. Underneath the bed, in drawers, are all his jerseys, with names and numbers on the back. It is the shrine of all his stuff.

McGwire will be a special card, he had said in the store.

"If he breaks the record this year," he said, "I'll know I had this card from the start."

"It's good that it has a cover on it," he said. "You have to take care of your special cards."

This would be the season when baseball would get into his heart, the way baseball still can; the way it always has in this country, for boys like this. Alex would turn eight in April, a few weeks after Opening Day. He would play on his first Little League team. And this would just be the time in his life when the spark was lit for him. It would happen for his brothers, too, just more with him. Things go deep with Alex. In all the best, bright ways, baseball would go deep with him in the summer of 1998.

Like some McGwire home run that would never stop rolling.

It would not just be one thing, between this day in spring training and the end of the World Series. It would not just be the home runs, or all the games the Yankees would win, or the afternoon when he saw Ken Griffey, Jr., and Alex Rodriguez in person for the first time, or the manager of the Mets, Bobby Valentine, coming over to wish him happy birthday when he sat down close to the field at Shea Stadium with his friends.

It would not just be his first team, or uniform, or putting on catcher's gear for the first time, or buying the Mike Piazza mitt with his own money, or making baseball card deals with the adults who own and operate his favorite card stores; or the way he would close his door at night, when he didn't know I was on the other side, and do imaginary play-by-play of the big-league games he was playing inside his wonderful head:

"There is a long fly ball from Alex Lupica. . . . It could be a home run. . . . It IS a home run! . . ."

It would not be all the backyard games he invented, usually in the early evening after his supper, Wiffle ball games of home-run derby over the fence around the swimming pool, or all the fly balls I would feed him at the fence, the pressure all on me to make a perfect throw so he could leap against the fence and take an imaginary home run away from someone.

It was all of it, starting now, with the McGwire card in his right hand and McGwire on the field in front of him.

"He's going to hit one today," Alex said to his brothers.

We were in right field at Roger Dean Stadium, the Cardinals' new spring training home in Jupiter, Florida. Cardinals against one of the season's expansion teams, the Tampa Bay Devil Rays. The opponent held no real interest for my kids. Neither did the Cardinals, for that matter. They were here to see McGwire, in this sweet spring training place, everything new and trying to look old, because that is the trend in baseball now, at places like Camden Yards in Baltimore and Jacobs Field in Cleveland. It was the same in the spring. Places like Jupiter built ballparks like these and lured teams like the Cardinals away from Al Lang Stadium in St. Petersburg, an ancient capital of spring training, as ancient as the population of St. Petersburg.

And Jupiter got lucky, here at Roger Dean, hard by I-95 off Donald Ross Boulevard.

In the spring of '98, Jupiter got McGwire, who had hit 58 home runs for the A's and Cardinals the year before, who had become the biggest action hero in baseball since Babe Ruth. The stands were full this day because they would be full every day for McGwire, and everyone was here for the reason my sons and I were here:

He might hit one out today.

Maybe he would go deep.

The simplest things always bring us back. The promise of sports, the pull of it, is always the same for fans: We show up wanting this year to be better than last year. And we want to be a part of that. If this year was better than last year for Mark McGwire, even just a little better, a handful of home runs, he would get to 60, which was the best Ruth ever did, back in 1927. A couple more and he would beat Roger Maris's 61, hit for the '61 Yankees. That was the magic number now, for baseball and all sports:

Sixty-one.

Nobody had to tell me.

The spark had been lit for me that summer of '61, the summer of Maris and Mickey Mantle both trying to break Ruth's record. They were together for most of the summer and then Maris had pulled away at the end, finally passing Ruth on the last day of the regular season.

We were living in Oneida, New York, then, about twenty minutes east of Syracuse. Yankee Stadium was five hours away by car, and so it was on the other side of the world for me. My father and I followed Maris and Mantle on the radio, and on the Syracuse television station, Channel 3, that carried some of the Yankee games in those days. No ESPN then. No cable. No color television for us. I remember the season in black-and-white. I turned nine that spring. It was my first season in Little League.

That was my home-run summer, the way this would be a home-run summer for my sons.

I followed Maris and Mantle through the voices of Mel Allen and Phil Rizzuto. There were other voices for the Yankees, and on the Game of the Week. I can only hear Allen and Rizzuto. When I would finally go to bed, exhausting the last possible angle to get one more inning from my father, he would promise to leave me a note on the floor of my room. And would:

Maris hit another one. 42.

Mantle 1-for-4, no home runs.

Yanks, 5–2.

Or whatever it was. I would find the notes in the morning.

The whole season felt like morning.

So home runs started it for me, too.

I told Mel Allen about how it happened for me that summer. We were at a table in the media dining room at Yankee Stadium. Maybe it was a year before Allen died, maybe more than that. He would still show up for special occasions at the Stadium, still do a few innings in the broadcast booth when asked; almost until the end, he was the marvelous voice of the syndicated *This Week in Baseball* television show, talking over the highlights of the week and still making the whole world feel as if it were still in Little League.

I would sit with him every single chance I got. I never got tired of hearing that voice. I would even think about having him sign something for me, though I was never much of a collector of autographs, even as a kid. But then I thought: How could he possibly ever autograph all those nights when he made me feel as if the balls Maris and Mantle were hitting were landing at my front door?

"The way you felt about '61," he said to me that time, "that's the way we all felt."

The old man, past eighty by then, smiled at me and said, "That was the year Roger and Mickey made boys out of us all."

Now all this time later, in the Florida sun, I was with my sons, to watch the new home-run hitter. Sometimes sports is a big wheel that keeps turning and finally takes you all the way back to the beginning.

Before we had come inside, we had stopped to buy things. Christopher, who would turn eleven in September, had bought a miniature bat and Zach, five going on six, had bought a baseball.

The store had been rush-hour full even a few minutes before the first pitch. This is a time in sports when the obsession and fascination for the stuff—one that would turn into a national obsession about what would happen to the home-run balls McGwire and Sosa would hit on the other side of the season, in September—had become more important than the games, a day like this at the ballpark, when the kids would see McGwire in person for the first time the way they would see Junior Griffey later.

But then we were inside. And even on this day in late March, in the exhibition season when the numbers didn't count—before the numbers would become everything—all you had to do was move through the crowd to understand that McGwire's presence, in uniform, in person, had done something to the place. A switch that would be thrown every time he came out of the dugout, and then moved from the on-deck circle to home plate.

More than the other two, Alex watched every move McGwire made. The way he took his practice swings. The way he stared out at the pitcher. Even the way he spit. Alex always notices everything. The morning after the second Mike Tyson–Evander Holyfield fight, he was watching the tape of it with his brothers, not knowing anything about what had happened the night before. And the moment, the exact moment, when Tyson bit Holyfield the first time—before Holyfield hotfooted his way out of the clinch and before the announcers even realized what had happened—Alex turned to me and said, "He bit him."

I had needed the replays the night before to see it.

"What did you say?"

"Tyson bit him."

At Roger Dean Stadium now he said, "He's bigger than he was before."

"Who's bigger?"

"McGwire."

I pointed out that he'd never seen him in person before.

"He's bigger than on his rookie card, Dad."

The stuff. He had McGwire with the A's, when McGwire looked to be about half the size he is now.

Alex nodded solemnly and said, "He has new arms."

We had started out in seats behind first base, but we spotted the patch of green grass down the first-base line, past the area the Cardinals were using for a bullpen at Roger Dean. It looked like a picnic lawn, with blankets spread out and people bringing food over from the concession stand out there. The move was booked when Christopher saw the Cardinal right fielder end an inning with a running catch and then toss the ball to one of the kids hanging over the fence.

So we went out there and sat on the grass in the early innings. This was as close as any of my sons had been to a game, the field right in front of them. Spring training baseball is always more available, the way minor-league baseball is. McGwire looked huge at first base.

The first time I had been this close to big-league ballplayers was in Cooperstown, New York, at the tiny ballpark there where they play an annual exhibition game the Monday of the Hall of Fame inductions. The Stadium was too far away from Oneida, but Cooperstown was not. And one year the Yankees were in the game.

I don't remember how long the game lasted that day. Just that the Yankees looked as if they were close enough to touch, before a hard rain came and washed the game out and made everybody run out of the ballpark and through the streets of the movie-set town for cover. The fans ran for cars, the players ran back to the hotel.

My father and I ended up under an awning with Bill "Moose" Skowron, the Yankee first baseman. I don't remember a word of what was said. My father made small talk with Skowron, who had a crew cut and a face as broken-in as his glove. It was a way of keeping Skowron there a few moments longer, before he caught up with his teammates.

He was as big to me as McGwire was in Jupiter.

Much bigger than his baseball card.

MCGWIRE GAVE ONE A RIDE HIS THIRD TIME UP.

We had decided that the one more inning before we left was this inning, the fifth. McGwire would come up in the fifth, against Rolando Arrojo of the Devil Rays.

And so, for the last time for us that day, there was the current that hitters like McGwire have always sent through ballparks. Big guys have always brought the place to a stop, made you watch, all the way back to Ruth. Mantle and Maris did it, Hank Aaron did it. Darryl Strawberry, with the Yankees by now, did it the first time he ever had a bat in his hands at Shea Stadium, as a kid for the Mets.

They make you watch even when they miss.

McGwire didn't miss Arrojo. All these months later, I cannot tell you what the score was at the time. But I can tell you about the sound the ball made on McGwire's bat, even from where we were down past first base. And the way we jumped up, because all of Roger Dean Stadium was up. And the way my sons' eyes were suddenly full of the sky, just on the chance . . .

The ball missed by a foot.

Maybe two feet short of going over the wall in left center field.

He had to settle for a double, and so did we.

The ballpark sat back down and we began to move toward the exit behind home plate, while McGwire stood grinning at second base, grinning at his near miss and maybe just the joy of being able to hit a ball that hard and know you didn't get it all.

Alex took one last look before we left. At McGwire, dwarfing the Devil Rays' second baseman. At the field. At the day.

"You think he can do it?"

I said, "You mean break the record?"

He nodded.

"I actually think he's going to do it and Griffey's going to do it, too."

Alex said, "If they both break it, who wins?"

"The one with the most home runs wins."

He took my hand and we caught up with his brothers. From behind us, from inside Roger Dean Stadium, we heard the start of a cheer, then a break in it, then a much bigger cheer. It was either a ball in the air that had fallen in the outfield, or maybe a ball in the air that had made it all the way out. It was the sound of baseball, though.

Summer begins early sometimes.

OUR FIRST OFFICIAL DAY WAS ABOUT MCGWIRE. We had come to see him get his swings. We didn't know in Jupiter in the spring that he would hit 70. We didn't know that by September, on the other side of the season, it wouldn't just be one spring training park coming to a stop for him the night he broke Roger Maris's record, it would be the country.

But the feeling we had that September night, my sons and I knew that feeling already, because we took it away from Roger Dean Stadium and kept it, like Alex's card.

In October, watching the World Series one night, I said to him, "Do you remember who the Cardinals played when we saw them?"

"Devil Rays," he said.

"How come you remember that?" I said.

His eyes briefly left the television screen and he gave me that look kids give you, when you don't understand the video game they are playing or *Rugrats* or the card trade they have just made with one of their brothers.

"Because I do," he said.

Because no matter how old you are or how much you have seen, sports is still about memory and imagination. Never more than during the baseball summer of '98, when baseball made everyone feel like a kid again, when it felt important again. At a time in American life when we all would feel as if a law had been passed requiring us to look through some White House peephole at Bill Clinton and Monica Lewinsky in a charming little study off the Oval Office, baseball would feel as if it were saving not just the country, but the whole world.

For one magic season, everybody's eyes would be full of the sky.

I never thought I would have a better baseball season than the one I had in '61, not just because of the home runs, but because of what I thought was the best Yankee team I would ever see in my life. Now I saw more home runs, and a better Yankee team.

It was McGwire and Sosa and Ken Griffey, Jr., at least until McGwire and Sosa pulled away from him the way Maris had pulled away from Mantle once. It was a strikeout pitcher for the Chicago Cubs, a twenty-year-old named Kerry Wood who could strike out 20 batters in a game.

David Wells of the Yankees would pitch a perfect game for the Yankees in May, the first perfect game in Yankee Stadium since Don Larsen in the World Series of 1956. Wells has the tattooed body of a bouncer and tells anybody who will listen that Babe Ruth is his hero. Ruth wore No. 3. Wells wears 33. He likes late New York nights and closing the bar as much as Ruth did. He did not look like the most likely candidate for a perfect game. Neither did Larsen in '56. Larsen, with his tired saloon face, was known for drinking and late nights himself, as much as for his pitching. Before the '56 Series, his lifetime record was 30–40. In 1954, his record with the St. Louis Browns had been 3-21. After the perfect game against the Dodgers, this was the lead Joe Trimble wrote about Larsen in the New York *Daily News:*

"The imperfect man pitched a perfect game."

Forty-two years later, another imperfect Yankee pitched a perfect game. Somehow everything is connected in baseball. One story, one event, always reaches back for another. You understand the season you are watching because of something that happened before. So perhaps it figured, or came from the stars, that Larsen and Wells came from the same high school, Point Loma in San Diego.

You couldn't make up a season like this.

Sosa would join the home-run chase in June, when he hit 20 home runs in the month, another record in the home-run summer. Now this wasn't just about an American-born home-run hero like McGwire, but one from the Dominican Republic, too. It is where Sosa got off a bus from Santo Domingo when he was sixteen years old and showed enough promise to a Texas Rangers scout named Omar Minaya that Minaya signed him to a $3,500 contract. A bus ticket worth maybe five dollars American became a ticket to the dreams that all kids like Sosa have. The same dreams McGwire had growing up in California. Somehow they would arrive at the same moment in baseball history, as if they were supposed to meet here all along.

McGwire and Sosa hit. Kerry Wood threw. Cal Ripken, Jr., finally took a day off, after sixteen years. He was thirty-eight the night he did it. Tony Gwynn was also thirty-eight in the baseball season of '98, and would have sat down himself because of aching knees and a ruined Achilles tendon, but Gwynn was limping toward one more World Series, his first since he was a baseball kid in 1984.

"I've always dreamed about one more," he said. "All the years when people told me to leave San Diego, go someplace else, even my dad, I knew I could get back. I wouldn't let go of that damn dream."

You always hope this will be your year. You always hope this year will be better than last year. That has always made old men young in baseball.

And it was not just honorable old baseball men. And it was not just the big leagues in '98. For one week in August, before everything was home runs, before all the morning conversation in America was about who did what the night before, the country would be charmed and thrilled by a group of kids from Toms River, New Jersey, winning the Little League World Series in Williamsport, Pennsylvania. Somehow it was perfectly fitting, like two perfect-game pitchers from the same high school in San Diego, that the Toms River kids hit five home runs of their own to beat Japan in the finals.

They will always remember this as their own home-run summer, then.

Two weeks after Toms River beat Japan, the Yankees brought them to Yankee Stadium. It was a night when David Wells would pitch into the seventh inning with another perfect game, maybe just because anything was possible in baseball now. But three hours before that, here was Todd Frazier, a pitcher and shortstop for Toms River, standing in front of the Yankee dugout, looking all around, trying to take in the whole place at once, a ballpark that seems skyscraper-high when you stand on the field, as Frazier did now with his teammates. Yogi Berra once described the first time he ever saw it, on a trip down from a submarine base in New London, Connecticut, where he was stationed during World War II. Berra said, "It was just this big beautiful place for baseball."

On this night in 1998, Todd Frazier nodded and said, "This is exactly the way it's supposed to look."

He could have been talking about the whole season.

His and everybody else's.

THERE IS NO ONE WAY TO LOOK AT A SEASON LIKE this, the way there is no one view of Yankee Stadium that properly explains the place. There is the view from the field, and from where

Yogi finally sat for eighteen years, behind home plate. There is the view from the outfield, where Ruth played, and Joe DiMaggio, and Mickey Mantle. Paul O'Neill, the Yankee right fielder for their two World Series in the nineties, says that sometimes he will be out in right field during batting practice, allowing himself to daydream, and he will look down at the place where he is standing out there and think, "Ruth."

Meaning, Babe Ruth stood where I'm standing.

"I feel like a kid," O'Neill said.

Everybody did, from the first pitch in March until the last out of the World Series between the Yankees and the Padres. For one season out of everybody's memory, everybody's imagination, everybody was young. The light of the season reflected through us all, ballplayers and ex-ballplayers, managers and broadcasters, Little Leaguers and Hall of Famers, parents and children, the fans at the ballpark and the ones connected to it by television or radio.

These are my own reflections of this one splendid season, from the crack of McGwire's bat in Florida in the spring to the ball in Tino Martinez's glove in Qualcomm Stadium in San Diego the night the Yankees won their twenty-fourth World Series, finishing off the Padres in four straight games. It is the reflection of home-run hitters and high school coaches, legendary Yankees and Yankees with cancer, old home-run hitters and old friends of Roger Maris's, scouts and Little Leaguers and Bobby Thomson, who once made what is still regarded as the most famous baseball swing of them all.

All the light that reflected off all the diamonds in the greatest baseball season America had ever seen.

More than anything, this is a book about my father and my sons, a golden thread stretching from 1961 to 1998, from Maris to McGwire, from the notes my father left me on the floor of my room to the ones I left for my sons, all the way through October, through the last game and the last out for the Yankees:

McGwire, 45.

Sosa, 41.

Yanks win!

Love, Dad.

JACK BUCK IS THE SEVENTY-FOUR-YEAR-OLD PLAY-by-play announcer for the St. Louis Cardinals. He is a voice for kids in the Midwest, even now, the way Mel Allen was my voice in the fifties and sixties, when I was growing up in upstate New York. Buck finally stayed around baseball long enough to see a man hit 70 home runs in a season, and tell people all about it on the radio.

Once, ten years before the summer of '98, Buck was calling the World Series for CBS. And in Game 1 of that series, maybe he thought he had made the most famous home-run call he would ever make. It was the ninth inning at Dodger Stadium, and the Dodgers had been behind all night against the Oakland A's, who that year featured a big kid at first base—though not nearly as big as he would become—named McGwire.

There are always connections from one season to another, held together by the same golden thread.

Finally, it was 4–3 Oakland in the ninth, two outs, the great relief pitcher Dennis Eckersley pitching for Oakland. Eckersley walked Mike Davis. Now Kirk Gibson, who wasn't supposed to play because of his ruined knees, came limping out of the dugout and made one of the most famous swings in Series history, beating Eckersley and the A's with a two-run homer that really won that Series for the Dodgers right there, like a first-round knockout in a heavyweight fight.

Ten years later, with the Red Sox in New York to play the Yankees in September, Eckersley, still pitching in relief for the Red Sox at the age of forty-three, still an important player on a team headed for the playoffs, would talk about what it was like to stand on the mound that night, watch the ball disappear, watch Gibson begin that hobbling, shambling trip around the bases.

"It was like an out-of-body experience," Dennis Eckersley said.

This is what Jack Buck yelled to the country that night, before Gibson began that trip around the bases, one that seemed to take about an hour and a half:

"I don't believe what I just saw!"

Jack Buck hadn't seen anything yet.

None of us had.

• *one* •

April

OFFICIALLY THE REGULAR SEASON BEGAN FOR MARK McGwire and the Cardinals in March. The thirty-first of March, to be exact. It was just a trick of the calendar. The baseball season is supposed to begin in April. So for McGwire, April was beginning early this year. Maybe to give him a jump on Ruth and Maris.

Maybe he could hit a ball out of one month and into the next.

But the beauty of Opening Day, in March or April, was the same as it had always been, unchanging and enduring, like the unchanging appeal of the home run. It is the same for everyone, the ones who play, the ones who watch. The ones who watch from the dugout.

"It's the unknown," Cardinals manager Tony La Russa said. "It's always the unknown."

It was the same for him this season as it had been for all the seasons of his baseball life, first as a player, then as a manager. The unknown. The excitement. The anticipation. But mostly the mystery about all the months to come, the longest season we have, one hundred and sixty-two games plus the playoffs, if somehow you were one of the eight teams who survived the 162 and were able to advance. La Russa had seen it all. He had won it all with the Oakland A's and twice been upset in the World Series, first by the Dodgers in '88— mostly because of Gibson's home run against Eckersley—then by the Cincinnati Reds in 1990. That was another Series that seemed to have been altered by a Game 1 homer, this one from Eric Davis, a bomb to dead center in the very first inning off A's ace Dave Stewart. The Reds won that game, and somehow the A's, led by McGwire and Jose Canseco, the Bash Brothers, were never the same after that.

Three times La Russa had gone the distance with what everybody saw as a great baseball team. Three times La Russa's A's had come into the World Series as the favorites. Only once had they won. In the two Series they had lost, the A's had been able to win only a single game.

Tony La Russa knew about the unknown in baseball.

Now came a different kind of Opening Day for him. La Russa did not have the best team this time and he knew it. Maybe the '98 Cardinals could steal the National League's Central Division. Two years earlier, even before the trade for McGwire, the Cardinals had won the Central and then led the Braves three games to one in the National League Championship Series before the Braves had come back behind the pitching of Tom Glavine and Greg Maddux and John Smoltz. The '98 Cardinals, even with McGwire, weren't nearly as good. Too many questions with the starting pitchers. Too many questions about depth. Even La Russa had to know he would need luck—and maybe more trades like the one that had brought him McGwire the year before—to make it to October this time.

You would watch his Cardinals across this summer because of McGwire, who was supposed to break the home-run record. He had hit 58 the year before; no right-handed hitter in baseball history had ever hit more. Now he was supposed to get Maris, even though McGwire was thirty-four at the start of the season, and only Willie Mays and Johnny Mize, the Big Cat who had played for the Cardinals and Giants and Yankees, had ever hit more than 50 home runs in a season at such an advanced baseball age.

La Russa wasn't worried about McGwire's age. He knew it meant nothing to McGwire, who felt he was just coming into his real prime as a home-run hitter, as a thinker at home plate. It was as if he had been preparing for this shot his whole life, from the day La Russa had first put him into the A's starting lineup for good, back in 1987.

"It was the mental toughness that would be so striking for me, all the way through," La Russa would say when it was all over. "It was the ability to put himself inside this box, focus completely on each at bat, four times a game, every game. Mark is stronger mentally than physically. And physically, he's ridiculously impressive, so mentally he's from another planet."

McGwire had hit 110 home runs the previous two seasons. Fifty-two in 1996. Fifty-eight in '97. Of those 58 the year before, 34 had been hit for the A's before the trade to the Cardinals, the one that had reunited him with La Russa. Twenty-four had been hit after the trade. He'd had only two months as a Cardinal in the books, and already he was considered the greatest power hitter in the history of a storied franchise, one second only to the Yankees in World Series won, even if the Cardinals were a distant second (twenty-three for the Yankees at the start of '98, nine for the Cardinals). The city had fallen in love with McGwire, especially after he got there and decided to sign a new contract without ever going near a free agency that probably could have paid him more, much more, than the $9.5 million a year the Cardinals were paying him.

During the off-season, McGwire had attended one of those Fan Fests that big-league teams hold during the winter, and had signed more than three hundred autographs.

For free.

It only made him more of a giant. More like Babe Ruth. Only Ruth in 1920 and '21, then again in 1927 and '28, had ever hit more home runs in consecutive seasons than McGwire had hit the previous two seasons, even moving from the American League to the National. So McGwire had finally become the right-handed Ruth, even if he had not made it to 60 yet.

On this Opening Day, La Russa remembered the beginning for McGwire, eleven years before in Minnesota. Back then, when McGwire had been a skinny rookie, the job for La Russa had been finding a way to just keep the kid with the big club. Get that bat in there, see what happened. See if he could hit some out early, so that both he and the manager who believed in him from the start would never have to look back.

But Sandy Alderson, the A's general manager, was worried that McGwire wouldn't get enough at bats; that is why there was so much talk all spring about having McGwire start the season in the minor leagues. The A's had another prospect, Rob Nelson, at first base. They had a former batting champion, Carney Lansford, at third base, which removed the option of moving McGwire over there.

"I'll find him at bats," La Russa told Sandy Alderson in April of '87. "Let me worry about that."

McGwire hit some out early. He never looked back. La Russa never looked back. Eleven years later, Sammy Sosa would spend an entire summer calling McGwire "the man." Mark's the man, he kept saying. How can I be the man when Mark's the man? He's the one who's going to break the record. He's the one who's going to win the race. But the first race for McGwire, the first time he was mentioned with Ruth and Roger Maris, was the first year. He hit 49 home runs that year, even if he broke down in the stretch. He was twenty-two and a rookie, and it all caught up with him in September. But the previous rookie record for home runs was 37; McGwire shattered that the way kids hit baseballs and shatter neighbors' picture windows.

No American Leaguer had hit more than his 49 since Maris had hit his 61 in '61 and Mickey Mantle had hit 54.

From the start, from the time Tony La Russa believed in him enough to find him those April at bats, McGwire had been a man to watch. Everyone had waited for the one season when it would all fall into place for him, and maybe for baseball. Now everyone, starting with La Russa, McGwire's friend and manager, believed that season had arrived. There had been all the seasons when McGwire's promise seemed gone, when he struggled with a bad back and with foot injuries. In 1991, McGwire hit just 22 home runs, had a batting average of .201 going into the last game of the season. La Russa sat him down. He had seen too much from McGwire. He was the first to trust the greatness in him. He wasn't going to let him finish a season with a batting average under .200.

Always, La Russa believed McGwire could come back.

He had come all the way back. La Russa had left Oakland for St. Louis in '96. He watched from there as McGwire hit 52. After the trade in '98, La Russa had seen McGwire make his first serious run at 60.

Now he was supposed to close the deal, once and for all, close the books on Ruth, close the books on Maris. And in the first game, of the new season, in this early beginning to April, he watched from the on-deck circle as Ramon Martinez of the Dodgers walked Delino DeShields, the Cardinals' second baseman, with two runners already on base for the Cardinals in the bottom of the fifth at Busch Stadium.

Bases loaded for McGwire.

The first game suddenly organized around him the way the summer would.

In so many ways, the beginning would be the same as the ending, the last day of March like the last day of the regular season in September. It was just that no one knew that yet, not in St. Louis or anywhere else.

"So now Mark is walking up there and there is just this unbelievable anticipation," Tony La Russa said. "Everyone in the crowd is saying, 'You're the man. We expect you to deliver.' "

The crowd saying exactly what Sosa would say all summer.

"How can a guy come through with that pressure?" La Russa said.

McGwire delivered. There were 47,972 people in the stands at Busch Stadium yelling for him to come through, and he did. Martinez threw, and McGwire murdered that pitch over the left-field wall.

No. 1.

It was the first Opening Day grand slam in the history of the St. Louis Cardinals, who would end up winning, 6–0.

"It's an awesome feeling," McGwire said that day. "How can you not get chills?"

La Russa smiled afterward and said, "I would have settled for a walk."

"Opening Day, bases loaded, the modern-day Babe Ruth comes up, hits a grand slam," Cardinals third baseman Gary Gaetti said.

By the end of the season, Gaetti would be traded to the Cubs, end up playing with Sosa. No one had a better view of '98 than Gaetti. Except for Tony La Russa, who would have the best seat in the house, every day of the long season, every swing. Every single moment like this, from the first moment on.

When it was all over, La Russa still looked back on Opening

Day with some wonder. He still sounded like a kid talking about McGwire, six weeks after the last home run. Still talking about the season that made kids of us all.

"There were so many times all year when I said to myself, 'How did he do that?' " La Russa said. "That was the first."

McGwire did not just set out after Maris with a home run.

But with a grand-slam home run.

Game on.

The blue line means you are a Yankee.

You walk in from the street at Yankee Stadium, the players using the same entrance as the media, and you walk down a flight of stairs and then if you are walking to the Yankee clubhouse, you turn right and follow the blue line that takes you all the way there. If you are walking to the visitors' clubhouse, you go left. A red line.

On this day in April, as the Yankees play their first home game of the season, they come down those steps and follow the blue line that other great Yankee teams have followed, the one that usually takes them all the way to October. Most of the players on the '98 Yankees have made the right turn before. Just not all of them. Chuck Knoblauch, who will become famous later in the year for a botched bunt play in the American League Championship Series, has come over to the Yankees in a trade with the Minnesota Twins during the winter. Knoblauch, a second baseman, has already been through spring training with the Yankees and opened the season on the West Coast with them. But he still has not been a Yankee at Yankee Stadium.

Until today.

Until today, when he had come to this place before, he had taken a left turn and walked the red line.

"I always wondered what it would be like to take this walk," Knoblauch would say later. "Walking the blue lines makes it official."

Now it was ten minutes to another season at Yankee Stadium and the elevator doors opened at the basement level and here came Joe DiMaggio, here to throw out another first pitch of another home season at the Stadium, walking the blue line himself. There were two security men with him, and a member of the Yankees' promotional staff trying to tell him something. DiMaggio nodded his head and walked slowly in the direction of another Yankee season, part of more than a line painted into the Stadium floor, part of the most famous line in the history of the sport, one that goes back to Babe Ruth.

Knoblauch had officially become a part of that on this day.

Of all the living Yankees, DiMaggio is the head of it.

He wore a blue blazer and gray slacks and a white shirt with a red tie. The arthritis, which has been eating away at him for years, had bent him over slightly. He was eighty-three years old on this day, would turn eighty-four in November. He was born a year before Frank Sinatra. In a month, Sinatra would finally pass away at the age of eighty-two. And then the most famous of our living legends, maybe our most famous celebrity name because it has been a famous name in this country for seven decades, would be Joseph Paul DiMaggio. On the cuffs of his shirt were these words:

"Yankee Clipper."

"I'm a little late getting down here," he said. "So many people upstairs today. They all wanted some baseball stories."

He smiled.

"I told them I had at least a few to tell."

The old man shrugged and said, "The ones I can remember, anyway."

He first showed up at this place in April of 1936. The Yankees won the World Series that year. DiMaggio wore that World Series ring, with its blue setting, on his left hand still. Later in his life he would have all his other Series rings stolen from his New York apartment. There were a lot of rings. DiMaggio played thirteen seasons for the Yankees, played in ten World Series, won nine, over time became one of the mythic heroes of American sport, because of his stoicism, because of his grace. More than Ruth before him or Mantle later, DiMaggio *was* the Yankees. He made baseball look so easy, and so did they. Sixty-two years after his debut in center field, after he first ran across that grass, he had become the centerpiece of all the Opening Day ceremonies.

Here, again, was the great DiMaggio. That is how Hemingway, with whom DiMaggio used to drink at Toots Shor's in the old days, referred to him in a famous passage from *The Old Man and the Sea*.

The great DiMaggio, here in another April.

One of the security men behind him said, "Do you know where you're going, Mr. DiMaggio?"

Without looking back he said, "I believe I do."

He walked away from the elevators and then down the long narrow hallway past the media dining room and then another left and walked past the Yankee clubhouse. On the door to the clubhouse is a plaque saying that this is the Pete Sheehy Memorial Clubhouse, honoring the late, legendary Yankee clubhouse attendant who went all the way back to Ruth. Of all the Yankees who passed through this room, Sheehy probably spent more time with DiMaggio than any of them, because DiMaggio was always more comfortable in some back room than sitting in front of his locker, available to the reporters. The story is that DiMaggio would show up for the game and the first thing he would say was simply, "Cup of coffee, Pete," and disappear to wait for Sheehy. The two of them would sit and drink coffee and smoke and get ready for another baseball day at the Stadium.

At the end of the ramp leading down from the Yankee dugout, someone said, "Cup of coffee, Pete."

DiMaggio smiled again. He does not smile easily and can be an angry and cantankerous old man when the press and public are not around. According to a circle of friends that gets smaller as he gets older, he is in constant pain. But there is something about Opening Day that brings out the best in him, the way it does almost everybody. No one knows the thrills this Yankee team will provide, that by the end they will be called a DiMaggio of a team because of their own cool, almost detached, grace and excellence. There is just the thrill of the whole thing beginning again in New York, in what is still the Capitol Building of the game.

DiMaggio poked his head inside the Yankee clubhouse, which he heard had been remodeled over the winter, becoming even more elegant than the austere place he remembered.

"Everything's new today, isn't it?" he said.

He was tossing a baseball in his right hand.

"Anybody want to warm me up?" he said.

The sun and the noise and music was at the head of the runway. It was time for DiMaggio to go up there. He walked up the steps and into the sun as Bob Sheppard, the Yankee p.a. announcer, introduced him, as he always does, as "the greatest living ballplayer." DiMaggio, who seems to get a little closer to home plate with each year, throws a strike to Yankee catcher Joe Girardi and then waves to the crowd with both arms. It is a familiar snapshot from the day. He disappears down the dugout and back into the shadows.

Once he could run all day on this field, and hit balls out of sight, when right-handed hitters had to hit them out of sight if they wanted to hit home runs to left and center at Yankee Stadium. Now one pitch seemed to exhaust him. He was out of breath by the time he sat down in a folding chair near the clubhouse door.

"That's the most exercise I'll get all year," he said.

When he was ready, he walked the blue line back toward the elevators. The doors opened and DiMaggio stepped inside. When he did, he found himself in the middle of all the players from the United States women's hockey team, which had just won a gold medal in the Nagano Olympics. They were all kids, college kids mostly. Just about all of them were born a quarter-century after DiMaggio played his last game for the Yankees in 1951. But as soon as they saw him, all conversation stopped in the elevator. It was as if a rock star had walked in there.

Hockey girls, swooning over Joe D.

They all piled out at the loge level, where the Yankee offices are, and the entrance to owner George Steinbrenner's suite and private box. Suddenly cameras appeared, and baseballs for DiMaggio to sign. He can be prickly about that, because for years he has commanded a small fortune for signing his name to baseballs and bats and other memorabilia. He has been able to make a very nice living for himself, just for being the great DiMaggio. I have seen fans rudely present balls to DiMaggio in settings like these, then watched him turn, get back into the elevator and disappear.

But today he seems to love it all. He signs and poses and enjoys the fuss the hockey players make over him. Maybe it is an old man's vanity. Maybe it is Opening Day, making even him feel young.

Katie King, one of the players, introduced herself and said, "I just wanted you to know that our coach always used you to motivate us, Mr. DiMaggio."

He asked how. The security men, in a panic because they know how much DiMaggio usually hates crowds, are trying to get him inside the Yankee offices, but he isn't going anywhere.

King said, "Before our games leading up to the Olympics, when we'd go from city to city, he'd always tell us to make sure to have a 'Joe DiMaggio day.' "

"And what exactly is a 'Joe DiMaggio day'?"

"He said that one time, late in the season after the Yankees clinched the pennant, somebody wanted to know why you played so hard that day, in a game that really didn't mean anything. And you said there might be people in the ballpark that day who had never seen you before, and you owed them your best."

"It was against the St. Louis Browns," Joe DiMaggio said.

He posed for a few more pictures, one with Cammi Granato, the team captain. He signed caps. Granato leaned up when it was time for them to go and kissed DiMaggio on the cheek.

He still had the baseball in his hand.

"It's like meeting one of the monuments from the outfield," Katie King said to Granato.

I watched DiMaggio go through one set of doors and then another and remembered a day three years before, when I took my father out to the monuments in the outfield.

It was the weekend Mickey Mantle died. My father was visiting from New Hampshire and he had gone in with me on Sunday morning for the taping of a television show. There would be ceremonies honoring Mantle at the Yankee game that day, to be played against the Indians. I wanted to write a column about Mantle, and growing up in the fifties and sixties when Mantle was the center fielder at Yankee Stadium, when Mantle was the greatest Yankee and the player we all wanted to be. I decided I wanted to go out to Monument Park in the morning, when it was quiet out there, before the whole media world would want to go out and look at Mickey Mantle's plaque.

I called Buck Showalter, then the Yankee manager, and asked if he would go out there with me. He said he would. I told him I had my dad with me. He said that was fine, bring him along.

My dad hadn't been back to the Stadium in thirty-five years. The last time he had been here, in 1960, he had seen Mantle with his own eyes. Now he was back here, on the emotional day when the Stadium would say goodbye.

We parked and walked across Ruppert Place and through the players' entrance and down the stairs, and now my dad walked the blue Yankee line down to where we were meeting Showalter, outside his office door. I thought Buck would take us all the way down the long hall, heading behind home plate and down toward left field, staying inside until we got to Monument Park.

"Let's go through the dugout," he said.

At nine o'clock on Sunday morning, the three of us walked up the steps and onto the field at Yankee Stadium. My dad was seventy-one at the time. He stopped and looked around at the Stadium, at the blue seats and blue walls, the amazing green of the outfield grass, the size and sweep of it all, all at once. Someday I would have my sons on this field with me, on a morning like this.

But first my father, seeing it the same way they would, seeing it for the first time all over again.

When he got to center field, he stopped again.

I would remember this on the day Paul O'Neill told me the story about standing in right and thinking about Ruth.

"DiMaggio," my dad said.

We went into Monument Park, and Buck and I went to Mantle's plaque and talked for a while and I took notes for my column. My father looked at all of them, taking his time, reading the words. When he got to DiMaggio, he just stayed, until Buck Showalter said it was time for him to get to work.

We walked back across the outfield, then the infield, into the Yankee dugout. My dad shook Showalter's hand, thanked him for the day. The manager of the Yankees went inside. We went back to the dugout, because my father said he wanted one last look.

Like one of my kids asking to watch one more inning, one more at bat.

We stood on the top step and Bene Lupica, seventy-one going on seven, said, "I was finally on that field."

His Joe DiMaggio day.

Later that month:

There were eight- and nine-year-olds everywhere in the gym at New Canaan High School. Alex's first day of Little League. There would be no game today, just a workout later on a field a few minutes away. But this was the first time he would be with his team—the Ontarios—and meet his coach, Mr. McFeely.

More important, this was the first time he would get his stuff.

Orange cap with the "O" on it.

Orange uniform, No. 11, with the name of his team's sponsor, RK Irrigation, on the back.

Later in the day, we would go to our local Bob's Sports and pick up his white baseball pants.

The gym was ashout with kids' voices. There were balls being thrown, rolling all over the basketball court. There were black jerseys and red jerseys, the Senecas and the Mohawks and the Iroquois. In one corner of the gym, one team had left a whole pile of baseball gloves while the kids went off to get their jerseys.

"I want number two," Alex said in the car.

"Derek Jeter," I said.

"Do you think I should play shortstop?"

"The coach will let you know."

"Shortstop or catcher," he said. "Do you think they'll have catcher's equipment?"

"For the season," I said. "Probably not today."

"Catcher's masks are getting as cool as goalie masks in hockey," he said. "Did you ever catch?"

"I told you, I only played second base."

"I could play second base and wear eleven."

I said, "Chuck Knoblauch."

"Eleven would be okay," Alex said.

When Cliff McFeely handed him No. 11, Alex smiled and gave me a thumbs-up, then went to play some catch with the rest of the guys.

I knew from our neighbors what a good league this was for kids Alex's age. If you are one of the coaches—and I had signed up as an assistant coach—you pitch to the kids on your own team. There are no walks. But there are strikeouts. By the end of this particular Little League spring, I would understand that there is no greater pressure in sports, none anywhere, than having a two-strike count on your own son.

I watched Alex run off in his orange No. 11. Found myself standing next to Coach McFeely, who was also commissioner of the league. I had heard from friends about what a hero he was to these kids. Across the season, I would see for myself.

"Isn't this a great way to get ready for baseball?" he said.

"You aren't just talking about Little League, are you?" I said.

"No," he said, "I'm not."

I told him, "I know this sounds incredibly hokey, but if they show any interest at all in baseball, I feel like it's our duty to encourage them."

"What part of that is supposed to be hokey?" Cliff McFeely said.

The gym was full of baseball. It was not just fathers and sons, because there were mothers here, too. The fathers take all the bows in sports, and it is the mothers who are the shuttle service from practice to practice, game to game. Dream to dream. But here was all the promise of a new season, all the high excitement of that, the gym sounding like a ballpark on Bat Day, or some other giveaway day, because all you could really hear were the voices of the kids, from every corner of the gym and the morning. The mothers shook their heads at the wonder and chaos of it all, the fathers remembered their first baseball Saturday morning, when they were the ones getting the uniforms, when their gloves were in the great baseball pile.

No one in this gym knew how wonderful the major-league season would be, how baseball would suddenly become fashionable again, even cool, after all the years, all the seasons when it had been pushed to the side by the cool of Michael Jordan and pro basketball, and the national obsession with pro football on Sunday afternoons. But the dads in the gym just knew they loved baseball and hoped their sons would love baseball. It was as simple as that.

There was a makeshift studio set up near the free throw line. That's where the photographer took the team photos, and the individual shots for the baseball cards. The fathers in the gym never had anything like that. But this was 1998. And times had changed. You could pay around $30 for a complete set of color photographs with your son's picture on them.

When it was Alex's turn, he stood in front of the blue curtain with a bat on his right shoulder, orange cap on his head, just the "1" from No. 11 showing on the back of his uniform. " '98" is in the top left-hand corner, his name is at the bottom. And I can tell you what is on the back of that card because I have it here in my wallet, with Alex's autograph on it, just because he felt he should autograph his card to his old man:

Alex Lupica, New Canaan Baseball
#11
Fav Pro: Derek Jeter

Team: Ontarios
Coach: Cliff McFeely
Position: Shortstop/2nd
Age: 08
Height: 4
Weight: 50
Throws: Right
Bats: Right

The card is starting to get a little worn already, after just one season in my wallet. I am thinking about putting it between plastic covers, like Alex's Mark McGwire card.

Alex is right.

You've got to take care of your special cards.

In April . . .

The home-run leaders for the first month of the '98 season are Mark McGwire, Ken Griffey, Jr., and Vinny Castilla of the Colorado Rockies, all of them with 11.

Sammy Sosa has six for the month.

In the National League, the Braves are four games ahead of the Mets in the East, the Brewers and Astros are tied for first in the Central, a game ahead of McGwire's Cardinals. The Padres are already five games ahead of the field in the NL West. In the American League, the Indians are in first in the Central Division, the Rangers are three games ahead of the Angels in the West.

The Yankees finish April with a record of 17–6, just a half-game ahead of the Red Sox, who are 18–8. In addition to all the home-run possibilities, there is also this possibility: a Yankees–Red Sox summer. After all the seasons, it is still the best rivalry in baseball, perhaps in all

*pro sports in America. It is New York vs. Boston, it is Harry Frazee, the
Red Sox owner, selling Babe Ruth to the Yankees, it is the fact that the
Yankees had won twenty-three World Series from the time they got The
Babe and the Red Sox had never won another.*

All that jazz.

*Now, at the beginning of '98, it seems that the Red Sox had a
team that might be able to stay with the Yankees. But there is also a
feeling of dread in Boston, because the fans can already see Mo
Vaughn, the team's star of the nineties, moving toward the door. He
isn't on his way to the Yankees. Just somewhere else. Anywhere except
Fenway Park. There is bad blood between him and Dan Duquette, the
Red Sox general manager, and has been for a while.*

*Vaughn had hit 44 home runs with 143 RBIs, a batting average of
.326, in 1996. In '97, even battling injuries and a couple of bad
slumps, he had finished with 35 homers and 96 RBIs and a batting average of .315. But he is to become a free agent after the '98 season. Duquette had not yet been able to come up with enough money to head all
that off, keep him with the Red Sox. When Vaughn was arrested for
drunk driving during the off-season (on his way home from a topless
bar in Rhode Island, just over the Massachusetts line), he felt Duquette
acted like a prosecutor instead of a defense attorney, even before
Vaughn went to trial and was acquitted. It just made Vaughn more
angry toward Duquette and, it seemed, more determined to make this
his last season in a Red Sox uniform. The year before, the Red Sox had
lost Roger Clemens when the Blue Jays had offered Clemens a lot more
money. Now it seemed Vaughn was about to be lost from Fenway forever.*

*Lost from what has forever seemed like the star-crossed franchise of
baseball.*

*But if Vaughn would not be around for '99, at least he gave
everybody hope about '98 on his own Opening Day at Fenway. The
Mariners led the Red Sox 7–2 that day. But the Red Sox loaded the*

bases in the ninth, and Nomar Garciaparra singled to make it 7–4. Mariners manager Lou Piniella brought in Paul Spoljaric to face Vaughn.

Spoljaric threw Vaughn an 0–1 fastball and Vaughn hit a grand slam and the Red Sox won 9–7.

"You always want to be in that situation," Vaughn said afterward. "I wasn't looking to hit a home run, that's something that just happened."

Had been happening since he had come to the Red Sox from Seton Hall, and had made them believe he might finally be able to break what was known in Boston as "The Curse of the Bambino." Him and his Ruthian uppercut. Him and that big burly body of his. Body by Babe.

On the first day, he gave them plenty of hope in Boston. It always seems to start out that way in Boston. . . .

two

May

THEY HAD WGN, THE SUPERSTATION OUT OF Chicago, on cable now in Grand Prairie, Texas, so at least the coach could catch some of the game if Kerry Wood did anything at Wrigley Field.

Randy Heisig, who had been the assistant coach at Grand Prairie when Wood pitched there, didn't care about watching the local news out of Chicago. He certainly didn't care about watching *I Dream of Jeannie* reruns, or reruns of *Coach* that seemed to play all day long. WGN meant Cubs games. WGN brought Wrigley Field to Grand Prairie. And put Randy Heisig in Wrigley Field when Wood had the ball.

And Kerry Wood had the ball today, May 6, against the Houston Astros.

In the afternoon, WGN would take Randy Heisig to that game.

It was only Wood's fifth big-league start. A month before, Wood had been pitching for the Iowa Cubs, Chicago's Triple-A team in Des Moines. On the telephone one night he had told Heisig that with a little bit of luck, and if he struck out enough Triple-A hitters, he might get called up to the Cubs in June. Maybe the All-Star break at the latest.

If he pitched like the kid that he was, twenty and just three years out of Grand Prairie, he still figured he might get called up to the Cubs in September, when the rosters in the big leagues expanded, and a lot of kids like Kerry Wood got their first taste of the big time.

Then things had happened, because they always do, and the season can change even before anybody gets out of April. There is no blueprint, not with a season as long as baseball's. There is no game plan. So one reliever got hurt for the Cubs, and another, Terry Mulholland, had to leave the starting rotation and go to the bullpen to fill a hole. Now there was a hole in the month of April for Wood to fill.

All of a sudden he had four starts for the Cubs in the books. Nothing spectacular. But he had shown enough to show he belonged. He was 2–2. He was struggling with his control, his breaking ball especially. Sometimes he didn't know where his fastball was going, either. Still there had been these stretches of games when he had lit up the park with the power of his right arm. Every once in a while, a new kid like this comes along, all the way back to Bob Feller, who was the first baseball teenager to show up in major-league baseball ready to strike out the world.

So on this day, Wood would go up against the Astros. He would go up against a batting order that included Craig Biggio, Derek Bell, Jeff Bagwell, Moises Alou. It was as tough and formidable a stretch of hitters as there was on any team anywhere.

Heisig wanted to see how his kid handled himself.

From his office, he called Martha Jordan, the librarian at Grand Prairie High School. Heisig told Martha Jordan he would like to watch the Cubs–Astros game on the library television, the only one in the school with cable.

She said, "Fine, you bring the popcorn."

On the day when the season would come roaring into the library at Grand Prairie as big and loud as Wood's fastball.

At about 1:10 in the afternoon, a few minutes before Wood's first pitch, Heisig walked into the library. For the first few pitches of the game, he would be alone. With the game. With his own high school memories of Wood. He had known from the first day, the first time he ever watched the kid throw with his own eyes, that Kerry Wood was the best he would ever coach. If you coach, you always hope there will be one like this to show up at the field one day, come walking into the gym.

And now here he was, what felt like twenty minutes from his last game at Grand Prairie, on the library television, going through all the mannerisms Heisig knew by heart, going into that big delivery.

A few minutes later, after Wood had struck out Craig Biggio to start the game, Heisig was joined by two of his varsity players, Chris Cohen and Richard Bridges. When Wood had been a senior at Grand Prairie, in the spring of 1995, Cohen and Bridges had been on the team with him as freshmen. Three years later, another April, amazing for these kids to watch, there was Wood on the same field with Mark Grace, and Henry Rodriguez.

And the Cubs' right fielder, Sammy Sosa.

Wood struck out Derek Bell in the first as well.

Then Jeff Bagwell.

In the second inning, Buddy Berry, the Grand Prairie principal, showed up in the library, which had now become a corner of the bleachers at Wrigley Field, just not as loud.

Yet.

In the second, Kerry Wood struck out Jack Howell and Moises Alou.

He got Brad Ausmus in the third, after allowing a single to Ricky Gutierrez, the Astros' shortstop.

"How many strikeouts?" Buddy Berry asked.

"Six," Randy Heisig said. "Six in three innings. And he hasn't walked anybody, that's the big thing."

At two o'clock, Heisig had to leave for softball practice. He would have to miss some of the game, but only until that night. Wood would call the way he usually called after one of his starts, and he could fill Heisig in on the last four or five innings of what looked to be the best day he had had yet in the majors.

Ninety minutes later, Martha Jordan sent one of the kids from the library out to the practice field, telling him to catch the coach before he left softball for spring football practice.

"Coach," the boy said. "Miss Jordan said I should come out here and tell you that Kerry has struck out sixteen batters already and the game isn't over."

He looked at his watch. He imagined the defensive ends already on the field, waiting for him.

"He can't have struck out sixteen," Heisig said. "That's just not possible."

Not knowing that this would be the baseball season when the impossible became possible, almost everywhere.

Even in Grand Prairie, Texas.

"Well, that's what Miss Jordan told me to tell you," the boy said.

Heisig went to football practice, his head full of baseball. And memories of Kerry Wood. He had spent only one season at Grand Prairie, transferring there from Irving MacArthur, a high school in the same district, a district that stretches from the eastern edge of Fort Worth to the western edge of Dallas. It didn't endear Wood to his teammates at MacArthur, or fans of the MacArthur team. But MacArthur wasn't much of a baseball school, and Grand Prairie was.

Wood was going places.

His teammates at Grand Prairie included Kevin Walker, who would be drafted in the sixth round of the amateur draft by the Padres; Jeff Ryan, who went on to become a star at shortstop for Wichita State in 1998; and Jeff Dover, by now a quarterback in football and a star baseball outfielder at Texas Christian University in Fort Worth.

Wood went 15–0 at Grand Prairie. He struck out 156 batters in 81 innings. His team had a record of 33–4 and made it all the way to the Final Four of the Texas 5A playoffs, the state championship competition for the state's biggest schools. "Our kids would just sit on the bench and laugh," Heisig said, "knowing that the guys on the other team had no chance to hit the ball. Our catchers went through three mitts that season."

A bond developed between the coach and the fastball pitcher. Wood would go over to Heisig's house and watch ball games on television. One New Year's Eve, Heisig's daughter Abby sat on Wood's lap while they all watched bowl games. And in the spring of '95, after the Cubs had made Kerry Wood the fourth pick in the draft, Wood showed up at Heisig's house to ask for advice about his baseball future, which had come upon him much sooner than he had expected.

There were so many requests for interviews all of a sudden. Too much attention.

"I knew to get away," the boy said. "Where should we go bass fishing?"

Heisig gave Wood and his buddies three fishing poles and sent them off to his favorite fishing spot in East Texas, maybe seventy miles from Grand Prairie. Knowing that day how much Wood's world was about to change.

Three years later, a secretary from the athletic department came out to the football field to find Randy Heisig and tell him what Kerry Wood's fastball had just done to the baseball world.

"The game's over," the young woman said. "The Cubs won and Kerry struck out twenty."

She shrugged.

"Back in the office, they were saying it's some kind of record."

"I knew she had to be wrong," Heisig said. "There was no way. I told her he probably struck out thirteen or fourteen in all. She just didn't understand."

He finished practice. He went back to his office. There were three messages already. *The Dallas Morning News.* A local TV station. The *Austin American-Statesman.* Wanting to talk about the record. Heisig knew his baseball history. He had already looked some things up, just because he knew the power of Wood's right arm. The possibilities. It was a baseball spring, after all, never too early to think about those possibilities.

It is a time in baseball for everybody to dream.

It had to be the rookie record.

Eighteen strikeouts.

It couldn't possibly be twenty.

Heisig called one of the reporters who had called him.

Now he believed.

He went home to watch the highlights on ESPN's *Baseball Tonight* show, which had become the town meeting of the sport, every night of the season, for everybody from Wrigley Field, Chicago, to Grand Prairie, Texas.

The head coach when Wood had been at Grand Prairie had moved on to another job. Heisig was still there. He was the coach who had coached Wood in high school. At school the next day, there were three radio reporters. Four television stations. "To this day, I can't tell you how many newspapers," Randy Heisig said. Newspapers from New York to Chattanooga.

Wood finally called Heisig a couple of nights later.

Heisig just laughed when he heard the kid's voice.

"What're you trying to prove?" the coach said.

"You know what the funny thing is, Coach?" Wood said. "I didn't even realize that I struck out twenty. I was just excited I didn't walk anybody. Remember how you always told me not to walk anybody?"

And that is how it started for Kerry Wood. You never know when it is your time in baseball. To hit home runs. To strike everybody out. He was just the latest to find out. A strikeout kid, striking out twenty in the spring, before the home-run summer.

"Coming out of high school, you just hope to get a chance," Wood said a couple of weeks later. "And coming out of high school, that chance isn't very good. It's all happened so fast, but I'm trying to grab hold and enjoy the ride."

Roger Clemens, another Texas right-hander with an arm like McGwire's bat, had always been Kerry Wood's hero. Now, in just his fifth major-league start, at the age of twenty, three years from Grand Prairie, Wood had tied Clemens's record for most strikeouts in a nine-inning game. He had struck out more batters in nine innings than Tom Seaver ever had, or Steve Carlton.

Or Nolan Ryan.

He had become the second pitcher in the history of baseball to strike out his age. The first since a seventeen-year-old out of Van Meter, Iowa, named Feller.

Wood, in May of '98: "To be compared to [Clemens, Ryan, Feller] this early really isn't realistic yet. I go out and do my job every five days, and if in ten years they want to compare me to those guys, I'll gladly accept it."

In a season when so many would charm, Wood was first. He turned down Jay Leno. He turned down David Letterman. No, thank you. Here was a bonus-baby kid in the hey-look-at-me culture of sports not looking to be an instant immortal, not looking to make a huge score off one magic day. The boy in him was safe, secure still.

Wood: "I don't care if I'm on the magazines and in the papers or if I'm on TV every day. To me, I would rather come to the field every day and have everyone forget about me and say, 'Who's that guy? Where did he come from?' And then just leave me alone."

In June, Randy Heisig made the trip to Wrigley Field to watch Wood pitch in person. Once against the Marlins, once against the Phillies. Against the Phillies, Heisig even saw Wood hit his first big-league home run, a ball he hit so hard the Phillies' center fielder never even turned around. Heisig sat in the stands and laughed the way the Grand Prairie kids used to laugh watching the high school kids on the other teams try to play the same game Kerry Wood was playing.

"I think he would play baseball for free," Heisig said that day. "I'm sure his agent would be mad at me for saying that. But I think he would."

Kerry Wood wears No. 34 for the Cubs. Nolan Ryan's number. In high school, Wood had worn No. 21. Clemens's number. He would have worn it when he got to the Cubs, but the number was already taken.

By Sammy Sosa.

THERE WILL ALWAYS BE SOME WHO BELIEVE THAT the great season began exactly where it should have begun, with McGwire's bat, with four home runs the first four games of the season, as if he had set the debate right there, once and for all, about whether or not he would finally make history, after two straight seasons when he had gotten to 50 home runs, after coming so close to Ruth and Maris in the '97 season.

But perhaps the first real explosion, a sudden and unexpected fireworks display, was the strikeout kid, not the home-run hitter. One afternoon at Wrigley when all that mattered was the sound of the ball in a catcher's glove, not the crack of the bat. This happened in Chicago. It happened in the second week of the National Basketball Association playoffs, Michael Jordan in the Eastern Conference semifinals, on his way to his third straight NBA title, his sixth in eight years. In other years, maybe in any year except this one, the only conversation in Chicago would have been about the Bulls. The only sports stars to talk about would be Jordan, Scottie Pippen, or Dennis Rodman, the Tattooed Mutant Ninja Forward of pro basketball.

On this week, they were talking about Kerry Wood not just in Chicago, but all over the country. It wasn't just Heisig, the coach, who needed *Baseball Tonight* on May 6 to see exactly what Wood had done to the Houston Astros, it was everyone. A twenty-year-old pitcher had stolen Jordan's headlines and Jordan's thunder in May, before the same thing would happen in June with No. 21 of the Cubs, Sosa, when he was the one who became the star of *Baseball Tonight*, almost every night, when he had a home-run month the likes of which no one had ever seen.

But for now, this week in May, it is Wood, out of Grand Prairie, Texas.

The Saturday after Wood's 20 strikeouts, Alex's team, the Ontarios, played the Senecas on a back field at the New Canaan Country School. It was one of those dream Saturday mornings, the day full of summer, the field full of kids. In Alex's league, everybody plays, everybody hits. Depending on who is away and who is sick, there are usually fifteen kids in the field, fifteen in the batting order. When I am pitching, and I usually pitch the first three innings, I look behind me sometimes and want to laugh, because all I can see are kids from the other team everywhere, and then this splendid chaos every time a ball is hit anywhere.

Sometimes the deployment of the infield and outfield troops takes longer than the baseball.

This is one of those games the kids on the Ontarios will talk about all season. They are behind 22–15 going into the bottom of the sixth, which is the bottom of the last in the league. They finally get to 22–21 on a double down the right-field line by Alex, and then Conor McDonough, the biggest boy on the team, a nine-year-old neighbor with a classic left-handed uppercut swing, hits one over everybody and everybody scores and the Ontarios win, 24–22.

After the game, while the kids are having their postgame snack, the coach, Cliff McFeely, and I are picking up helmets and bats and gloves. He has been a Detroit Tigers fan all his life. We have talked about it before, how the only team that scared the Yankees in '61 were his Tigers, led by a famous Yankee-killer of a right-hander named Frank Lary.

"Did you see that Kerry Wood?" he asked.

I told him I had, that my kids wanted to go to the card store that day, hoping that they might find a Kerry Wood card even though he had been in the majors for only five starts.

"There's something going on this year," he said.

There are always baseball days you remember, even in Little League. I could not tell you one other score for Alex's team, even though they seemed to win almost every week and end up a couple of games away from the championship. But there was something about this one game, this one morning. Maybe the excitement of the way it had ended for the kids.

"I mean in baseball," Cliff McFeely said. "I've been doing this a long time, and sometimes the only time I'd talk baseball all week would be with the kids. But this season is different. I can't explain it, but there's something in the air."

I pointed toward our bench, all the bright loud 24-to-22 activity there, the game already being replayed, the bottom of the sixth having become the top of the whole day.

"You ever wonder which one of these kids might turn out to be Kerry Wood?" I asked Cliff McFeely.

"You have to understand something," he said. "On mornings like this, they all are."

Maybe someday the reporters would come around and ask him about Conor McDonough.

"David Wells is three outs away," John Sterling said on the radio.

He is the Yankee play-by-play man on WABC radio. He has a wonderful voice, and often turns the most routine plays into opera. He is one of the characters of the Yankee season, a cartoon sometimes, but a lot of fun, like some Barrymore of baseball broadcasting.

"Three outs away from what?" Christopher says.

We were on our way home from one of Alex's baseball games, having dropped Alex off at a friend's house, still hoping we could catch the last couple of innings of the Yankees–Twins game on television. But it was obviously the ninth if Wells was three outs away from something. And there was something going on at the Stadium, because you could hear the excitement running through Sterling's voice.

I pulled the car over to the side of the road. My father would never do it when my mother was in the car. Just the two of us. Something big would be happening and he would find the first safe place to pull over and then do it. Then it would be the two of us alone in the car with Mel Allen, or Phil Rizzuto. I can remember the first time he ever did it, in the '56 maroon Dodge.

"You can't watch the game and watch the road at the same time," he'd say.

"But we're not watching the game," I would say.

"Sure we are."

Now Chris and I watched with John Sterling, even if we didn't know exactly what we were watching. A few years before, Chris and Alex and I were coming home from the United States Open tennis tournament on a Saturday afternoon when Jim Abbott was pitching his no-hitter for the Yankees. Abbott was the left-handed pitcher who had been born without a right hand and still managed to become a baseball star. I had met him when he was sixteen, to do a piece on him for *Parade* magazine. Abbott and I had played catch in front of his home in Flint, Michigan, so I could see how he was able to throw the ball and then get his glove out from under his arm in time to catch it. Just because Abbott was always something to see.

All that time later, we sat and listened on the car radio as he pitched a no-hitter for the Yankees at Yankee Stadium.

One more memory, reaching out for another.

Chris Lupica, who remembers the womb, remembered the day of Abbott's no-hitter, sitting in the car.

"You think Wells is pitching a no-hitter?"

"That must be it."

Wells gets the first out of the ninth. A pop to O'Neill, in right. Michael Kay, Sterling's broadcaster partner, once a baseball writer for the *New York Post* and the New York *Daily News*, talks about how Wells looks disheveled, as usual, on the mound at the Stadium. He talks about how the 49,820 at the Stadium are on their feet, focusing their attention on Wells.

Sterling says that Javier Valentin, the Twins' catcher, steps into the batter's box and takes ball one.

"You can hear the crowd groan," Sterling says.

In the car, pulled off to the side of Route 124, fifty miles from Yankee Stadium but right in the middle of this now, I say to Chris, "He's pitching a perfect game."

"How do you know that?"

"Because the crowd doesn't groan about ball one if he's just pitching a no-hitter. If they're worried about ball one, they're worried he's gonna walk him. David Wells has got a perfect game going."

That is exactly what he had going, on Beanie Baby Day at Yankee Stadium, the place crawling with kids. There always seems to be some kind of giveaway on Sundays at the Stadium. This time it was those little stuffed animals that were taking over the whole world the way they had taken over our house. Only by the ninth inning, everything had changed. Wells was trying to give away history. Forty-two years after Larsen's perfect game in Game 5 of the 1956 World Series, Wells was trying to make it twenty-seven Twins up, and twenty-seven down. Joe Torre, the Yankee manager, had sat in the upper deck, up above third base, for Larsen's game against Brooklyn. He was on a pass from St. Francis Prep in Brooklyn, using a ticket given to him by his brother Frank, who was playing for the Milwaukee Braves then. Joe Torre would say that he had come to root for the Brooklyn Dodgers that day, because he was a Brooklyn kid. By the end, he was the kid on his feet, rooting for history.

Now he sat in the Yankee dugout, alongside his bench coach, Don Zimmer. In the '56 World Series, Zimmer was in the visiting dugout at the Stadium, still playing for the Dodgers, rooting all the way until the last out, until Larsen struck out Dale Mitchell, for somebody to get on base.

"I rooted all the way until Yogi jumped into Larsen's arms," Zimmer said to me once.

Now he sat next to Torre on the Yankee side of Yankee Stadium and rooted for Wells.

My oldest son and I sat in the car.

Or maybe it was the front seat of my father's Dodge.

The count went to 1–2 on Javier Valentin.

On the radio, Michael Kay wondered if any player on the Yankee team really wanted the ball to be hit to him.

"They're all rooting for a strikeout," Kay said.

David Wells struck out Valentin.

Finally, John Sterling says it: "One out to go for a perfect game."

"You were right, Dad!" Chris says.

"Shhhh," I tell him. "Watch."

I have heard the tape plenty of times by now. I was trying to scribble in the car that day, because I knew the paper would want some kind of column on this. Later I would see all the pictures on television. But Chris and I saw the moment through Sterling and Kay. Chris will remember Sterling's voice the way I remember Mel Allen. The way I remember Rizzuto, on the last day in '61, calling No. 61 for Maris. This will be Chris's sound track. This will be a memory for him. This was all the magic of baseball on the radio. My radio.

My father's.

This is what it sounded like when Wells threw his last pitch to Pat Meares of the Twins, as the top of the ninth exploded in John Sterling's voice:

"Popped up! He's gonna get it! O'Neill . . . near the line . . . He makes the catch! David Wells . . . David Wells has pitched a perfect game. . . . Twenty-seven up . . . twenty-seven down! Baseball immortality for David Wells!"

I turned to Chris.

"You ready to go home, pal?"

"Not yet," he said.

We sat there a while longer, listening to the celebration, imagining the Stadium. When we finally got back on the road, Chris talked more about Jim Abbott. I explained to him about Larsen.

WHILE JORGE POSADA, THE YANKEE CATCHER, WAS running for Wells the way Yogi Berra ran for Larsen once, Berra was walking through the Pittsburgh airport. He had one of his sons, Dale, with him. There had been a baseball card show in Pittsburgh and now the two Berras were on their way to a late-afternoon flight back to Newark, New Jersey, knowing nothing of what was happening with David Wells.

On that day in 1956, after strike three to Dale Mitchell, Yogi Berra became one of the most famous black-and-white pictures in all baseball history. Larsen was the one who had pitched the perfect game, but somehow it was Berra, his catcher, No. 8, who became the perfect picture, leaping into Larsen's arms, nearly obscuring Larsen completely.

Now, in New York, it was Posada making what some catchers still call the Yogi run. Yogi didn't find out until he walked in the front door of his Upper Montclair, New Jersey, home about 7:30. No one on his plane had known about the perfect game, no one had said anything at the airport, he hadn't bothered to turn on the radio on his way home.

When he walked in the door, his wife Carmen said, "Did you hear?"

"Hear what?"

"David Wells pitched a perfect game for the Yankees. How could you not hear?"

Yogi Berra looked at her and said, "Carmen, there wasn't a radio on the plane."

He went right for the television and dial-flipped until he was able to find some of the highlights from Wells's day. And as he sat there, it became October of '56 for him. He found himself looking for Posada. Joe Torre would have his memories of that day, from the upper deck, all the way from Avenue T in Brooklyn. Zimmer would have his memories, and as soon as Wells got to the Yankee clubhouse, he would be on the phone with Larsen. Wells knew that Larsen had gone to Point Loma High School. His high school. Pretty soon the world would know, because it was part of the history of the day, part of the story.

Yogi Berra remembered his own day.

When he was the one with the best seat in the house.

A baseball ends up in Paul O'Neill's glove and it is not just one memory that explodes, like a voice on the radio, it is a million memories.

"That was the best it ever got," Yogi Berra said the next morning. "How could you ever beat perfect?"

He played fourteen World Series in eighteen seasons for the Yankees. He played his first in 1947, and he was on the Yankee teams that won five straight World Series between 1949 and 1953. He came in with Joe DiMaggio and finished with Mickey Mantle. He would manage the Yankees into the Series once, do the same with the New York Mets, go to four more World Series as a Yankee coach. But there is always one day. His day was Larsen.

The catcher in the perfect picture.

"As soon as my wife told me," he said, "I went right back to that day. How could you not?"

I asked him what he remembered, and he said, "Try everything."

Posada was in the Monday papers talking about how nervous he became as the game went along, how he felt as if he could hear his own heart from underneath his chest protector, even as loud as the Stadium had become by the ninth inning. I asked what it was like for Yogi in October of '56.

"It was a two-to-nothing ballgame, remember," he said. "Sal Maglie was pitching pretty good himself. Larsen only ended up throwing ninety-seven pitches. There was never any time to be nervous."

He said he did worry about a walk. He heard the groans from that Yankee Stadium crowd every time Larsen would throw a ball instead of a strike. He wanted Larsen to stay away from ball three, no matter what. Memories upon memories. Yogi talking in May of '98 about October of '56, and how he sat behind the plate that day and started thinking about another Series game he had caught in 1947. Bill Bevans had a no-hitter, a Series no-hitter, going for the Yankees that day, but he also walked the whole ballpark, in Yogi's words, ten walks on the day, and finally Cookie Lavagetto broke up the no-hitter with a double, beat the Yankees.

You start talking about Wells and end up with Lavagetto.

Memories bouncing off memories.

"A no-hitter is always special," Yogi Berra said. "But a perfect game is something that only comes along once in your life."

Now it had come along twice in the life of the Yankees, of Yankee Stadium. Twice the ball was in the hand of a pitcher out of Point Loma in San Diego. The manager of the Yankees had been in the park for both of them. So had Don Zimmer. Yogi Berra said he sees Larsen all the time. A few weeks after Wells's game, Berra and Larsen would make an appearance together in Kansas City for a pharmaceutical company.

I asked Yogi Berra if there had ever been a time in the four decades since Larsen's game when the two of them had been together and not talked about it at least once.

He laughed.

"We talk about it with each other. Then people want to talk about it with us, especially when we go to the bar. It was one of those things, you know? One of those things that happen in baseball that people talk about the rest of your life."

It is baseball and it gets in your life and won't get out. You sit in your car and listen to a game on the radio on a Sunday afternoon and then suddenly, it isn't your car or your season. It is a '56 Dodge, somehow taking you all the way back to the '56 season. It all seems perfect. And like Yogi says, how do you beat perfect?

In May . . .

At the end of May, the Yankees and Indians both begin to pull away in their respective divisions, both of them 7 ½ games in the lead.

The Rangers are 5 ½ ahead of the Angels in the AL West.

In the NL West, the Giants are within 2 ½ games of the Padres, the Cubs are two behind the Astros in the Central.

And the Braves are five ahead of the Mets in the National League East. Only in New York, Mets fans suddenly feel as if the race in the East is just starting, as if the whole season is starting all over again, because one week after the Dodgers shock baseball by trading catcher Mike Piazza to the Marlins, the Marlins turn around and trade him to the Mets.

Piazza is in the option year of his contract; the Dodgers let him go after he turned down a seven-year, $84 million contract offer (before 1998 is over, the Mets will hang on to Piazza by giving him $91 million for seven years, to that point the biggest deal in baseball history). The Mets wait a few days and then go right after him, for a lot of reasons, all of them having to do with the tremendous need.

The Mets have been out of the playoffs for nine seasons. They have been completely eclipsed in New York by the Yankees, even though the Mets twice owned New York themselves—in '69, when they were the Miracle Mets, and in '86, when they won 108 regular-season games and the World Series—the way the Yankees do now. Attendance at Shea, where the Mets twice broke New York attendance records in the eighties by drawing three million fans, is so low the ballpark sometimes feels as sad and empty as a vacant lot, even when the Mets get off to a good start, as they have over the first seven weeks of the '98 season.

But not today. Not on Saturday, May 23, when Piazza makes his Mets debut at Shea against the Milwaukee Brewers. There are 32,908 people in the stands, and five of them come in our car: my three sons, Chris's friend Andrew, and me.

The plan had been hatched that morning.

"If Piazza ever takes the Mets back to the World Series," I said, "we'll be able to say we saw his first game for the Mets."

The boys did not require much persuasion. They all wanted to invite friends, but it was Chris's turn, and so we drove to Shea in the middle of the afternoon—a four o'clock game—and were amazed at the traffic and the lines we saw at the ticket windows, the biggest walk-up crowd for the Mets in years.

There are many things that never change in baseball, and one of them is this:

One player can still change everything.

Piazza was not just the best-hitting catcher in baseball history already. In his first five full seasons in the big leagues, he had 167 home runs and a lifetime batting average of .337 and the last player to break in with numbers like those, in those two categories, was Joe DiMaggio.

When we walked through the Diamond Club entrance at Shea that day, Jimmy Murphy, a cop who has worked the door there forever, said, "You see those lines?"

I told him I sure had.

"It's like the old days around here," he said.

On Piazza's first day.

We sat high above third base. We were part of this amazingly happy impromptu baseball party. We cheered Piazza when he came out for the top of the first and got behind the plate and cheered him his first time out, even when he made an out. The people at Shea would soon be booing Piazza. "I'm not Superman," he said when he signed, but they wanted Superman and when he gave them less in July and August, he would hear it, but good, from his own fans.

Today they cheered every move he made, as loudly as we did above third base.

This is what hope sounds like, not just at a park like Fenway when Mo Vaughn goes deep on Opening Day, but any day that feels like a beginning. The place went wild when Piazza got his first Mets hit, a double. Nobody wanted to leave when the game was over and the Mets had won. Opening Day II at Shea Stadium. Sports at its best takes big places like New York and makes them feel like a small-town high school gym. It happened on this Saturday in May.

"They're going to catch the Braves, you wait and see," Alex said in the car, just because anything was possible now.

The next day, he went and got birthday money he had been saving for a month and we went downtown to Bob's Sports and he bought his Piazza mitt.

· *three* ·

June

PERFECT BASEBALL GAMES, PERFECT DREAMS.

"In my country," Omar Minaya said, "the dreams about baseball are as strong as they used to be in America."

He was born in the Dominican Republic, the way Sammy Sosa was, then he was raised in the Corona section of Queens, New York, in the shadows of Shea Stadium. First Omar Minaya lived on Ninety-ninth Street in Corona, then Ninety-eighth, then Ninety-fourth. So many of his friends were soccer players. On a Sunday in Corona, in Flushing Meadow Park, near where the United States Tennis Association's National Tennis Center stands, all you can see are soccer fields and soccer games, to the point where this always feels like the capital of all soccer in New York City.

"But I was going to be a ballplayer," Omar Minaya said.

His dreams traveled, all the way to New York City.

Minaya became a star catcher in high school, Newtown High in Queens. He was good enough to be drafted in the fourteenth round of the 1978 amateur draft by the Oakland Athletics, who would draft Mark McGwire six years later in the first round of the same draft. The Athletics liked Minaya's speed and converted him to an outfielder, and all of a sudden, as a kid, he was playing baseball for a living, Class-A ball, in Bend, Oregon.

And he got to Oregon and even there, even in Class A, he could see that he was out of his weight class. He saw what most of them see. He was fast and they were faster, he could hit and there were better hitters all around him. He thought he had an arm until he stood in the outfield and watched the other outfielders throw.

He thought he had power, and then the ones hitting before him and after him in batting practice started hitting the balls out of sight.

"You change your dreams fast," he said.

But he had been around the life now, even at this entry level. He loved the life. The life was everything he thought it would be, even if his career was not. He wanted to stay around. He was smart, and he was one of those players who impressed everybody by the way he could sit in the dugout and break down the game. By the 1985 season, Minaya was back in Class A, this time as a coach. But he was already scouting as well. If he couldn't be a baseball star, he would be the first from the Dominican Republic to be a general manager in the big leagues.

"I was every kid who did not want to let go," he said.

He was working in the Gulf Coast League for the Rangers when he got a call from a veteran Rangers scout named Amado Dinzey. And Dinzey told him about a skinny sixteen-year-old kid back in the Dominican who had a live bat and a big arm. Dinzey was not authorized to sign players; Minaya was. Dinzey told him to fly down as soon as he could, because the kid was available.

"This is where the Sammy Sosa miracle began," Omar Minaya said in the summer of '98.

It did not begin in June of '98, when Sosa seemed to hit a home run every day for the Cubs, every day for a month, suddenly taking the home-run headlines away from McGwire and making them all about him. It really started the last week of May. From May 25 through June 21, Sosa hit 21 home runs in 22 games. Maybe it was fitting, or just part of the magic of this season, that the streak ended on the first official day of summer. That all seemed like a miracle—at Wrigley Field and all across baseball.

Twenty-one homers. Twenty-two games. Minaya remembered a better one, from the summer of '85.

He was one of the first to see Sammy Sosa.

"I call it a miracle," he would say later, "because of how far Sammy has come to call these home runs. Mark McGwire, I am sure he comes from a very nice high school. Ken Griffey, Jr., he comes from a very famous baseball family. Sammy Sosa comes off a bus to Puerto Plata."

Sosa had been working out at a camp run by the Toronto Blue Jays, maybe the first big-league team to appreciate the baseball riches to be found in the Dominican Republic. The Blue Jays' camp was in Santo Domingo. Minaya arranged for the kid to take a bus from Santo Domingo to Puerto Plata. The tryout would be conducted in Puerto Plata Stadium.

Minaya picked Sosa up at the bus. The kid got off wearing his baseball pants, an old red baseball jersey with holes under the arms, and his baseball spikes. Also with holes in them. Sosa had his own bat.

"He got off that bus ready to hit," Minaya said.

By the 1998 baseball season, Minaya was assistant general manager of the Mets, his childhood team. As a child, he sat in the upper deck and watched the Mets of 1973 make an improbable run to the World Series. Now he had a big job in this same place. There were such big ideas for him about making the short trip here from Ninety-fourth Street and Ninety-eighth and Ninety-ninth. Dreams change.

Sosa helped change them.

"Some things never change," Minaya said. "Sammy Sosa still gets off the bus ready to hit."

He remembers so many details of the day. Mostly the red jersey, the spikes with the holes in them. And how Sosa was even skinnier than he had heard from Amado Dinzey. "Malnourished," Minaya said. "Is that the right word? I noticed some of the balls he hit to the outfield, they'd look like he had hit them very hard and then run out of steam. That to me was malnourishment. He was nearly six feet tall, even then. Maybe he weighed 150 pounds. But I noticed something else even more: the boy's bat speed."

Thirteen years later, Minaya was fast giving Dinzey the credit for spotting the baseball giant inside this boy; this boy who had a home-run summer like this in him. If there had been no excitement from Dinzey, there would have been no scouting trip back home for Omar Minaya.

Minaya admits that he did not see the slugger that Sosa would become, did not see 66 home runs in him, did not see what all the scouts saw at once with McGwire, even when he was a skinny kid. But he looked at the boy that day and saw the man.

"Right from the start," he said, "you could see how aggressive he was. There was a fire inside this boy. Did I ever think he was going to hit fifty home runs in a season, or even sixty?" A laugh. "Of course not. You remember, this was the middle 1980s in baseball, when we actually used to think thirty home runs in a season was a lot. I will tell you exactly what I told the Rangers. I told them I thought he could hit twenty-five to thirty. But fifty or sixty? They would have laughed at me."

He decided to offer the kid a contract. He went with him to the family home in San Pedro de Macoris. A one-bedroom apartment. In the presence of Sosa's mother Lucrecia, Minaya offered a contract of $3,000.

Before the mother said anything, the boy shook his head.

No.

"You don't want to sign?" Minaya said.

"Four thousand," the boy said.

"Three thousand is what we generally offer."

The boy said, "Four."

The sixteen-year-old boy, still wearing the old baseball jersey, the old spikes.

"Three thousand five hundred, then," Omar Minaya said.

The boy shook his hand.

"And that is how it began," Minaya said.

The next year Sosa was the one playing in the Gulf Coast League, on a team with Juan Gonzalez. The Rangers would eventually trade him, a terrible deal, one of the worst of all time, for an aging hitter named Harold Baines. Sosa went to the White Sox. The White Sox traded him to the Cubs. It was Larry Hines, the general manager of the Cubs at the time, who finally saw what Dinzey and Minaya had seen; Himes said he saw a player who could hit 30 home runs, steal 30 bases in the same season.

Now, in June of '98, when it was all supposed to be between McGwire and Griffey for the home-run crown, to make the home-run chase at Roger Maris, Sammy Sosa began to hit balls that would not come down. Once, he had been the kind of player who walked on the field and changed everything for a scout, became the player for which that scout would always be remembered, the way a man named

Tom Greenwade had become a part of the Mantle legend because Greenwade was the one who signed Mantle.

Now Omar Minaya was part of Sammy Sosa's story.

It was Sosa who had come out of the Dominican to become a baseball star, who would finally become one of the biggest stars in the world. It was Sosa who had lived out Minaya's own baseball dreams. If you are a player once you are always a player. Minaya did not want to have an office at Shea Stadium when he was growing up down the block, he wanted to have a locker, he wanted to be a Met, he wanted all the kids to know his name. But as the home runs kept coming for Sammy Sosa, he would feel as if there was a small corner for him in the home-run summer.

Just because what we were all seeing now, he had seen, in Puerto Plata Stadium.

What started in June would never stop for Sosa. The balls would never really come down. Even at Shea Stadium, Minaya would look out some nights and see all these kids wearing Sosa's blue No. 21, as many kids as he would see wearing Mets jerseys. He would see the kids on the streets of New York City with that No. 21, Sosa's name on the back in bright red letters, smile, shake his head.

"How can you call it anything but a miracle?" he said.

The whole stadium would come to a stop now when Sosa came to the plate. His at bats would be replayed, one after another, on the highlight shows at night. Soon he would have more home runs than Griffey. Soon it would be McGwire and Sosa the way it had been Maris and Mantle. Minaya watched it all, talked about it on the phone with Sosa sometimes. Remembering how the only sound in Puerto Plata Stadium had been the bat Sosa brought with him.

Remembering the red jersey with the holes in it. He couldn't remember the number, just the boy inside it.

Thirteen years later, the scout looked at the man and saw that boy.

Sosa would end up with 20 home runs for the month of June. Once, a million years ago, Rudy York of the Detroit Tigers had hit 18 in a month, and that had been the record until the night of June 25, an interleague game between the Cubs and Tigers, when Sosa hit his 19th of the month.

It had all been McGwire until now. People always wanted to see where Griffey was, but it had been McGwire's show all along. By June 30, he would still be in the lead with 37 home runs. But now Sammy Sosa, off that bus, out of nowhere it seemed, had moved into the spotlight with 33. He had asked McGwire to move aside a little. Smiling as he did, blowing kisses, as if this were all some kind of lark, as if he were the Little League kid hitting the ball over everyone on a Saturday morning.

McGwire and Sosa.

This was the month when the two of them became a team.

With half a season still to play.

With summer officially beginning on June 21. Sammy's number.

"I cannot believe this is happening to me," Sosa himself said. "It is like some kind of miracle."

Imagine that.

Also in June:

It was early, much too early to write anybody off, certainly not a baseball immortal, but the season seemed to have left Roger Clemens behind, the way the Yankees and Red Sox were leaving Clemens's team, the Blue Jays, behind in the American League East. Clemens is the best of his time in baseball, better than Greg Maddux or anyone, one of the great right-handed pitchers of all time. He is the whole package—power and control and fearlessness and durability—that Walter Johnson was. That Nolan Ryan was. Coming into the season, Clemens—hero to Kerry Wood, hero to all the young power pitchers of the day—had won four Cy Young Awards in the American League and knew that a fifth would allow him to make baseball history of his own in the summer of '98.

With a right arm for the ages, as dangerous and imposing a weapon in his sport as any home-run hitter's bat.

But on May 29, Clemens had a record of 5–6. He lost to the Cleveland Indians that night, 7–3. He gave up ten hits and four earned runs. He struck out nine Indian batters, got a little closer to 3,000 career strikeouts. And lost. He was thirty-five, would turn thirty-six in August. He was old enough in baseball that people wondered how much he had left, because people always wonder when you reach a certain age.

"When you're young and you slump, it's just a slump," Tommy John told me once. "When you're old and you slump, you're old."

But after May 29, over the last four months of the season, through his thirty-sixth birthday, Clemens would not lose another game. He would start 22 more games for the Blue Jays. His record for those starts would be 15–0. He would leave the rest of the field behind: the kid, Kerry Wood; Maddux, who also had four Cy Young Awards coming into '98, and in April and May seemed a sure thing to beat Clemens to No. 5; David Wells and David Cone of the Yankees; everybody. Clemens won his fifth Cy Young going away, and if they had only given out one Cy Young for baseball, instead of one in each league, he would have won it anyway.

The Blue Jays would make a late, futile run at Clemens's old team, the Red Sox, for the wild card in the American League. Mostly they were forgotten in the AL East. Except for The Rocket, Clemens, who every fifth day would make them important, because he was as important with the ball in his hand as he had ever been, even at an age when he was supposed to be losing something off his fastball.

Underneath the home runs, underneath the crack of the bat, was still the sound of Clemens's fastball in the catcher's glove. The sluggers weren't the only ones playing the big notes.

He was the McGwire of pitching, at the age of thirty-five.

Sosa took off in June of '98, but so did The Rocket.

IT WAS THE NIGHT OF JUNE 30, METS AGAINST THE Blue Jays in SkyDome in Toronto. Clemens against the Mets' ace, Rick Reed. And so it was another night of the season, in what would be a good long streak of them, when the Lupica boys got to stay up a little later.

As the first one, Zach, went past his bedtime, I saw my wife, Taylor, standing in the doorway of my study. The game-watching room in the house.

"Don't tell me," she said. "It's a baseball thing."

My wife is wonderful and tolerant and patient about sports, with her sons and especially with her husband. She drives to more practices than I do, sees as many games, not just baseball, but basketball and soccer and hockey. Again: Fathers take the bows in sports, get drunk on the romance of it all. Mothers, who usually have much better things to do, handle most of the transportation. But baseball, the depth of it, the importance of the balls and gloves and rituals and statistics and memories and cards and stuff—mostly the memories—has always been a mystery to her. She has always talked about it as if it were a gene passed down, but only from fathers to sons. Some trick of DNA. The Baseball Thing.

She loves basketball. Loves going to pro basketball games, especially when the Knicks are in the playoffs and Madison Square Garden seems like the main plaza of New York City in April or May. The baseball thing just makes her shake her head, smile. Now more than ever. When baseball was about to take everybody past their bedtimes again, not on a school night this time, but a camp night.

"It's the Rocket, Mom," Zach said, as if that explained everything.

"Oh," Taylor said, nodding. "The *Rocket.*"

"Against the Mets," Alex said.

Chris had the sports section from *USA Today* spread out in front of him.

"If he strikes out sixteen tonight, he gets to three thousand," Chris said. "For his career."

My wife smiled.

Shook her head.

"If it happens," she said to me, "maybe you should leave me a little note on my pillow tonight."

She looked at her three sons on the couch, left to right, smallest to biggest, staring at the television screen. Chris darker than the other two, but not by much. A woman at school had once told me that watching them get out of my car in the morning was like watching someone take apart a Russian doll, with smaller dolls packed inside, each looking exactly the same as the one that came before.

"The baseball thing," she said again.

"It *is* the Rocket, honey," I said.

"Tonight it's the Rocket," she said. "Tomorrow night it's somebody else."

It was the Rocket. It was the sound of the fastball, even coming out of the television as if we suddenly had Dolby sound in the game-watching room. It was the way he carried himself on the mound. As tall as Randy Johnson was, six feet ten inches tall, Clemens pitched bigger. He just did. Carried himself as if he were in a different weight class than everybody else. A McGwire of a pitcher. By 1998, he even had a bigger and better Web site than any other ballplayer: RocketRoger.com.

It was still better to watch him pitch, to remember what it was like when he was the kid like Wood, when he first threw his 20 strikeouts. When he was the kid to watch in baseball. He had arm troubles and he came back from them. He became a free agent and left Boston for the Blue Jays. And kept striking out all comers. And somehow, as he grew older, maybe because it happens to all of us as we grow older, he seemed to fall more in love with his own game, with the history of it, with his own place in that history. With all history, in fact.

When the Blue Jays are in Baltimore to play the Orioles, Clemens organizes trips for his teammates to the various monuments in Washington, D.C.

"Too many guys sit in their rooms watching cartoons," Clemens said one day during the summer. "But we have these great opportunities to see the country."

On the night of June 30, the Mets saw him. It was not the best game he would pitch all season. By the time Clemens would pick up steam in August, there would be shutouts against Seattle, and Minnesota, and Kansas City, on the night when Clemens struck out 18 Royals. Twelve years after he had struck out 20 Mariners, in April of '86, he would nearly get to 20 again.

But on a night in SkyDome when the roof was open and the wind blowing out toward the fences felt as if it could turn infield flies into home runs, on a night when the Mets' Reed gave up four home runs, Clemens—whose record was up to 8–6 by then—reminded everybody in the place, starting with the Mets, just who it was they were watching.

"My slider was good," he would say afterward. "My fastball was sharp."

Like Muhammed Ali saying he moved pretty good, was pretty sharp with the jab. On a night when even Clemens would talk about how small the wind made the ballpark look and feel, he brought size to the occasion, and weight. He did not get to 3,000 on this night. But he struck out eleven Mets, nine after the third inning. In the fourth, he struck out Bernard Gilkey and Brian McRae looking. He struck out Todd Pratt and Rey Ordonez in the fifth; Luis Lopez and John Olerud in the sixth; Edgardo Alfonzo in the seventh. In the ninth, he ended things by striking out Butch Huskey and Pratt again. The Mets were just the latest to find out what all hitters eventually found out against Clemens: the wind always seems to be blowing in when his slider is good, his fastball is sharp.

The outfield fences seem to be as far away as the moon.

"The funny thing is," Mets manager Bobby Valentine said, "I didn't think he had his best stuff the first couple of innings. But then, in the fourth inning, he threw a couple of fastballs away to Gilkey and then to McRae. Tom Robson, my hitting coach, is sitting next to me and I hear him say, 'Uh-oh.' "

Once, with the Texas Rangers, Valentine had managed Nolan Ryan at the end of Ryan's career, Ryan still striking people out at forty-two and forty-three and forty-four, already way past 3,000 strikeouts himself, defying all the laws of pitching, everything that is supposed to happen to even the best arms, the best fastballs, over time. Now he was seeing it again with Roger Clemens.

There are baseball sights that never get old.

"Nolan and Roger are the only ones I can think of who not only kept the arm strength and the velocity and the power as they've gotten older, but also became better *pitchers,*" Valentine said.

He had seen it when Clemens was young, when Valentine managed the Rangers and Clemens pitched for the Red Sox. He was seeing it again in June of '98. Seeing it good and clear in SkyDome as the game between the Blue Jays and the Mets went on.

Uh-oh, Valentine's coach had said.

"He gets that fastball going on the outside, and it doesn't just freeze hitters," Valentine said, "it paralyzes them. And he makes it look as easy as rolling a ball down a slide. It gets there so quickly and then the night belongs to him. He lights up the night and you can see hitters, even good hitters, just take the rest of the night off. He looks like a man playing against boys.

"He was always imposing, don't get me wrong. He always had that power. But when he was younger, that power was always up in the strike zone, sometimes out of the strike zone. He didn't have the control he has now. He certainly didn't have the control of the outside the way he does now."

Bobby Valentine, his head still full of June 30, 1998, talked about what you still see with Roger Clemens, what you still hear.

"It's like he comes with special effects," Valentine said. "It's not just the fastball coming at you like something coming down a chute. It's not just the one he throws that falls off the table. It's the sounds. There's the grunt for the fastball, and then there's the sound of that fastball away. Because he's not just throwing hard then, he's throwing it right to the catcher's glove, so the catcher doesn't have to move it at all. And when he does that, the catcher can catch it in a way that doesn't hurt his hand, up in the seam of the glove. So there's a definite pop you hear. And believe me, Roger's pop is different from everybody else's. It's like another thing that's unique to him."

A baseball thing.

In June . . .

The Yankees are ten games ahead of the Red Sox by the end of June, the Indians are 8 ½ games ahead of the Twins, the Angels are 3 ½ ahead of the Rangers in the AL West, in what will be a roller-coaster race for the two of them all season.

The Braves are 8 1½ games ahead of the Mets in the NL East, the Astros are now six ahead of the Brewers, the Padres are 5 ½ ahead of the Giants.

Thirty-seven home runs for McGwire, a few days before the bally-hooed home-run derby at the All-Star Game. (Griffey Jr., a reluctant participant right up until his first swing in Coors Field, will be the winner of the derby.)

Griffey Jr. and Sosa are at 33.

Andres Galarraga, Greg Vaughn, and the brilliant young Mariners shortstop Alex Rodriguez—on his way to a 40-home-run, 40-stolen-base season—have 27 home runs by July 1.

And then there is Juan Gonzalez of the Rangers. Only a three-game slump at the end of June prevents him from having 100 RBIs by the first of July. McGwire and Sosa chase Ruth and Maris in '98, Gonzalez chases an old Cub named Hack Wilson, who once drove in 190 runs in a single season. In both 1992 and 1993 (when he tied Barry Bonds with 46), the Puerto Rican–born Gonzalez had led the major leagues in home runs; once it was thought he might make a run at 60 himself.

Now he goes for a different magic number:

One-ninety.

Taking his hacks at that.

Maybe Gonzalez could even get to 200 runs batted in for a season, because it was that kind of crazy season in baseball, you could see it even halfway through.

"Juan Gonzalez is a monster," David Cone of the Yankees had said in May after facing Gonzalez, giving up a home run to him.

Two years ago, Gonzalez had hit five home runs in four games against the Yankees in the first round of the playoffs, nearly knocked the Yankees right out of October and the whole season by himself. In 1997, even though he missed much of the early part of the season with a thumb injury, he still finished with 42 homers, 131 RBIs. He had already been MVP of the American League once, and by the end of the '98 season, Gonzalez would be MVP again.

When Juan Gonzalez and Sammy Sosa were growing up together in the Rangers' farm system, in places like Sarasota and Gastonia and Charlotte, they never could have dreamed that they would ever be MVPs the same season. Back then, they were too busy trying to learn enough English so that they could order lunch on their own.

"When no one understood us," Sosa said, "we understood each other."

Talent knowing talent. The two of them always knew how to hit. A decade later, one chased Ruth, Maris, McGwire, the other chased Wilson. González had 71 RBIs by June 1, 96 by July 1, would end up with 157, to go with 45 home runs and a .318 batting average. In the last four seasons, between 1995 and 1998, Juan González had averaged one RBI per game. Five 40-home-run seasons for him by now, before he turned thirty.

Two Latin-born players winning MVPs the same year, making it to the same place, the same golden summer, from Sarasota, Gastonia, Charlotte. When no one else understood them, they understood each other. . . .

· *f o u r* ·

July

Not one Yankee makes the starting lineup for the All-Star Game, and somehow it is perfect. Like their season. As if the whole team and the whole season is David Wells against the Twins.

"We will be represented mightily on the All-Star Team," the manager Joe Torre says. "But no one around here is consumed with it. That's not our style."

Which had become the height of style in baseball. People were beginning to run through the record book the way the Yankees were running through the American League, the way legendary Yankee teams had always run through the American League, to find out if anybody had ever won 60 games out of their first 81, which would be the exact halfway point of this Yankee season. Only three had:

The 1902 Pirates, at 61–20.
The '07 Cubs, at 61–20.
The '12 Giants, at 60–21.

NOW THE YANKEES HAD A CHANCE, EVEN IF THE fans had not elected one of them to be a starting-position player in the All-Star Game, to be played the next week at Coors Field. As it turned out, the Yankees would have a record of 61–20 at the break, and somehow that fit the team, and the team's history, and the place. Just because the '61 Yankees had been such a storied team. And because Roger Maris had hit 61 that year.

It just seemed like the right number, for this kind of right-stuff team.

Other than the third baseman, Scott Brosius, who had come over from the Oakland A's, made one of those sweet trips you can make in sports from last place to first place, not one of the Yankees regulars was having what anyone could call a career year. Bernie Williams, the graceful center fielder, had been hurt. Derek Jeter, the shortstop, had been hurt. Tino Martinez, who had been such a solid rock at first base for three years, since replacing Don Mattingly at first base, had taken a vicious, intentional fastball in the back—like a knife in the back—from Armando Benitez of the Orioles, touching off a vicious brawl at Yankee Stadium. So Martinez sat down, too. The Yankees kept going. They had brought over Knoblauch from the Twins, put him on the blue line at the Stadium, but he hadn't been nearly the All-Star player, at the plate or in the field, the Yankees expected, even if he had finally given the Yankees a reliable enough leadoff hitter that they could move Jeter, a superb situational hitter, to No. 2.

The pitching had been splendid from the start, not just Wells, but everyone in the starting rotation. Ramiro Mendoza, a talented, skinny young guy with a mean sinker, had pitched beautifully from the start of the season but had now been replaced by Orlando (El Duque) Hernandez, the Cuban refugee, once the star of the Cuban National Team, who had escaped Cuba the previous December by a boat in the night. Hernandez, the half brother of Livan Hernandez—who had been the star of the '97 World Series for the Florida Marlins—had been in the minors. But then David Cone had been bitten in the pitching hand by his mother's Jack Russell terrier. El Duque was brought up from the Yankees' Triple-A team in Columbus for an emergency start, and pitched brilliantly, and soon Mendoza was in the bullpen and El Duque, with his high kick and assortment of spins, was the No. 5 starter.

Even a dog bite worked out for the '98 Yankees.

The starting rotation did not just get better, it got more colorful with Hernandez.

The Yankee bullpen suddenly was even deeper with the addition of Mendoza, who would have been an able and useful starter on almost any other team in the game.

The weekend before, they had played the Mets at Shea Stadium. For the past two summers, a Yankees–Mets series had been a huge event in New York City, first at Yankee Stadium in '97, now at Shea. Like some New York Subway Series out of the past. A retro weekend, in what was becoming a remarkable retro summer all over baseball. And even though the Yankees did not sweep the series from the Mets, won just two of the three games, they showed you exactly who they were, because just about everyone on the team contributed something, some sort of big moment. Because that is what the season had been since April. O'Neill had hit a three-run homer to change Friday night's game, and Martinez had hit one on Saturday.

On Sunday night, the last night, in a game shown nationally on ESPN—the biggest audience of Hernandez's life, at least so far—he pitched like a star for eight innings, threw 142 pitches, before the Mets finally won 2–1. And even when they were beaten that night, the Yankees wouldn't give up. In the last inning, Carlos Baerga was on third with the potential winning run. Brian McRae was on first. One out. The Yankees had to bring the outfielders way in, to give themselves a chance at Baerga on a short fly ball. Luis Lopez hit a long one to right instead, to the warning track in deep right. Usually in this situation, once the right fielder realizes the ball is over his head, he just lets it go, because he knows he has no shot from the wall to throw out a runner coming home from third.

Not O'Neill.

There has been no captain of the Yankees since Mattingly retired. O'Neill has become the unofficial captain, though. The heart and soul of this amazing band. In the 1996 World Series, the Yankees had taken the lead for good from the Braves by winning Game 5, 1–0. The last ball of that game ended up in O'Neill's glove. He was playing that Series on a ruined right leg, because of a torn hamstring. Sometimes you worried he would fall down trying to swing. Joe Torre worried about having him in the outfield in the ninth inning that night, but he felt that O'Neill deserved to be on the field, because of who he was, because of what he had meant to the team. With two outs and two runners on, a Braves pinch hitter, Luis Polonia, hit another ball that could have gone over O'Neill's head.

But somehow, even running on the bum leg, running toward right center, he caught up with the ball. A few strides before the fence. When he got to the fence at old Atlanta Fulton County Stadium, he threw a small left hook into it. A picture that had become a part of the history of the Yankees.

And so had one from the next year, Game 5 of the first round of the playoffs against the Cleveland Indians, the Yankees losing 4–3, one out away from the end of the season, the end of their short run as champions of baseball. O'Neill at the plate. Nobody on. He hit a line drive that seemed to get to the center-field wall at Jacobs Field, high off that wall. Just not high enough. Marquis Grissom picked up the carom and threw back to the infield, and here was O'Neill—on two good legs this time, but certainly no speed man on the bases— coming hard toward second, running for his life the way he had run for Luis Polonia's ball in Atlanta the year before.

It was an ugly slide, like something out of a bar league.

For a moment, you worried that O'Neill might miss second base entirely.

He didn't.

Safe.

The Yankees were still alive, but only for one more pitch, until Jose Mesa of the Indians got Bernie Williams on a harmless fly ball. In the Yankee clubhouse afterward, in the crushing silence of next season, of the first night of the long baseball winter, O'Neill stood in front of his locker and said, "Sometimes being a line-drive hitter sucks."

On a team where everyone hated to lose, no one hated it more than O'Neill.

Another No. 21 in baseball in the summer of '98, same number as Sosa.

Now, in another moment that told you everything about O'Neill and the '98 Yankees, he refused to give up on Lopez's ball. Refused to let go of the night, really. O'Neill caught it and stopped himself and angrily threw it back toward first base. The way you are taught. Play them right to the bus.

Baerga had tagged up and scored for the Mets.

Once he did, the game was technically over at Shea Stadium.

For everybody except O'Neill, who was throwing behind McRae, trying to double him off first base. We would find out shortly that even if he had, it wouldn't have mattered under baseball rules. But now McRae was scrambling back toward first and here came O'Neill's throw, and for this moment it seemed as if the umpire had called him out, which would perhaps have meant double play, inning over, game still tied at 1–1. . . .

The umpires conferred, signaled that the game was over and the Mets had won.

Not before O'Neill had scared the Mets and every Mets fan in the place or watching half to death.

Afterward somebody praised him for playing the game right to the end.

O'Neill glared at the guy.

"That's what you're *supposed* to do," he said.

His team played ball the way you're supposed to play it. The rebuilding of the Yankees in the 1990s had really begun with the trade that brought O'Neill to the Yankees from the Cincinnati Reds in November of 1992. Other tough veterans showed up that year, to team with Mattingly, already in place at first base, even if his career was in decline by then because of a bad back. The Yankees signed Jimmy Key as a free agent. They signed Wade Boggs, the great Red Sox third baseman. There was Mike Stanley, a backup catcher with Texas who came to New York and flourished as a player and team leader.

Now there were tough veterans like this all over the Yankee team, in every corner of the clubhouse. O'Neill. Catcher Joe Girardi. David Cone, the pitcher who had come back from an aneurysm in his pitching shoulder two years before. Darryl Strawberry, the veteran home-run hitter who had come back from just about everything. Knoblauch. Williams. Brosius. It was like the baseball version of the Count Basie Band. A team full of old-Yankee values and old-

Yankee pride. A DiMaggio of a team. Quiet and professional like the manager, Torre.

O'Neill was the leader.

But the kid at shortstop, Jeter, the kid was the star.

One Sunday morning in the Yankee clubhouse, Cone watches Jeter come bursting through the door as if on his way to make another great play in the hole.

"Being Derek Jeter right now in New York is about as good as it gets."

The kid is the one all the kids want to be.

OTHERS IN THE ROOM, IN THIS BAND, HAD WON other places, even before they had played for the '96 Yankees. Cone had won in Toronto. So had Wells. O'Neill had won with the '90 Reds. Knoblauch had won with the Twins in '91. Strawberry had won with the '86 New York Mets.

It was different with Jeter. He felt that all he had known as a Yankee was winning, the way other Yankee kids had all the way back to Ruth. He had won as a rookie in '96. He felt the '97 Yankees would have won if they had been able to finish the Indians off in Game 4 of that first-round series, long before O'Neill gave them their last hope, last loud roar, in Game 5. The Yankees were four outs away from winning the series in Game 4, but then Mariano Rivera had given up a game-tying home run to Sandy Alomar and the Indians won the game in the ninth, then beat the Yankees the next night and sent them home.

"You know what I thought about all winter?" Jeter said on a Sunday morning, three weeks after the All-Star Game. "I thought about how much I hated watching the Indians celebrate on the field after they beat us. Because I knew that should have been us out there. We were the better team. We just got beat."

"My shortstop is young in years," Torre the manager said. "But he is as old as the Yankees."

Jeter made kids like my Alex want to wear No. 2 to bed and place his autographed black-and-white Jeter picture in the safest and least-trafficked part of his bedroom. And he made the young girls swoon as if he were the baseball DiCaprio. Every time Derek Jeter would come out of the dugout and stand in the on-deck circle, you would see this sudden rush of movement in Yankee Stadium, as if the great old place had suddenly tipped in his direction. This was not just one at bat, it was all of them, all season, young girls and young women moving toward the field with cameras in their hands, wanting to get a shot of No. 2, who was No. 1 in their hearts.

Perfect games on this team, Cuban refugees, aging stars, a manager from Brooklyn, the most famous windbag owner in all of sports. A center fielder, Williams, whose grace was compared to DiMaggio's.

Jeter is the glamour.

He is the *GQ* cover boy for the Yankee summer.

He is twenty-four on this day.

"The kid," Darryl Strawberry is saying before Jeter shows up, "already has winning in his blood.

"Think about it," Strawberry said. "He's young, he's got all this game, he's got style, he's single, women love him to death."

Strawberry laughed.

"Hell," he said. "*We* love him to death."

In a season that made us all reach across all the years to find another season we thought was even half as good as this one, in a season that made baseball king again in America, Jeter was a perfect star for the Yankees. He seemed to come way out of the past, when the Yankees were bigger than anything in professional sports in this country and a star Yankee was what all boys wanted to be. When winning was all the Yankees knew.

By the time the Yankees would finish this regular season with a record of 114–48, Derek Jeter's record as the Yankee's starting shortstop would be 302–184. This was the way DiMaggio broke in, starting with the '36 season. His first three Yankee teams had records of 102–51, 102–52, and finally 99–53. The seasons were shorter than Jeter's in those days, DiMaggio's winning percentage was higher. But he would have one more win than Jeter. In Mickey Mantle's first three seasons, the Yankees won 292 games.

"I'm in the right place at the right time," Jeter says.

I mention that this is about more than timing and luck. He had stepped into the full-time job of Yankee shortstop in the spring of 1996, and had ended up Rookie of the Year and wearing a Yankee World Series ring.

"I know it is," he says. "But you can never overlook timing in sports. What if I'd been a young shortstop coming up in the Baltimore organization behind Cal Ripken? Or what if some young middle infielder was trying to break in with Detroit during all the years when they had Alan Trammell at short and Lou Whitaker at second? I remember getting a taste of the action when I got called up here at the end of the '95 season. It was my first time here and Mattingly's last year. Here's a guy who's been a great player for so long and that's the first and only time he makes the playoffs [the Yankees lost in the first round to the Seattle Mariners]. That's something you don't forget."

He had made his debut, his official debut as the Yankee shortstop, after playing a handful of games the year before, in April of '96 on a cold day in Cleveland against the Indians. Cone was the starting pitcher. All this time later, in this hot, amazing Yankee summer, Cone remembers the day after Jeter gets up from his locker and goes looking for something to eat, which always seems to be his first order of business upon entering the room.

"He hit a home run, I remember that," Cone says. "And he made this great, over-the-shoulder running catch against Omar Vizquel towards the end of the game. And I remember watching him that day and just thinking, 'Wow.' Since then he has never looked back."

Jeter had not been the starting shortstop in the All-Star Game because his friend Alex Rodriguez, another glamour-boy shortstop, was having a better year. Nomar Garciaparra, the brilliant young Red Sox shortstop, did not even make the team. It was already being suggested in New York that Jeter, because he was playing the same position as Rodriguez at the same time, might make it to the Hall of Fame someday without ever starting an All-Star Game.

Jeter absolutely did not care. The only thing that has interested him from the start has been winning today's game. As the Yankees continued to pull away from the field in the American League East, there were constant questions about how they would keep themselves motivated, knowing they wouldn't play a meaningful game until the first game of the playoffs. It was best not to go near O'Neill's locker with questions like these.

Or the kid's.

"Every day is meaningful for this team," he would snap. "We play every game like it's Game Seven. That's why we are who we are."

It was a good weekend for talk like this at Yankee Stadium. The day before had been Old-timers' Day. Of course, DiMaggio had been there, the last to be introduced. The old-timers were maybe the only ones who could understand a team like this.

The old-timers looked at the young man at shortstop and understood him completely. They were young like this once at Yankee Stadium.

JETER'S TEAM WON AGAIN THIS DAY. THE YANKEE record went to 73–26 for the season. There was no need to leave a note for the kids, because it was an afternoon game, they got to watch some of it on television.

And they watched Sammy Sosa hit No. 38 for the Cubs against the Mets in Wrigley Field.

Somehow, no one asked what had happened with McGwire, whose Cardinals were playing the Colorado Rockies in Denver, until Zach did, right before bed.

"Leave me the score of the Sunday night game and a note on McGwire," he said.

Zach:
McGwire. No. 44!
Dad.

In July . . .

Mark McGwire has 45 home runs at the end of July.

Sosa has 42.

Ken Griffey, Jr., has 41.

Greg Vaughn of the Padres is up to 38.

By now the Braves are 14 games ahead in the NL East, the Padres by 13 in the West. The best race is in the Central, where the Cubs are still just 3 ½ games behind the Astros. In the American League, the Indians are 10 ½ in front of the Twins, the Angels are a game ahead of the Rangers.

The Yankees are 76–27 through games of July 31, fifteen games ahead of the Red Sox, eleven games better in the loss column than the Braves or Padres, the best of the National League. In July alone, here are the records of the regular Yankee starting pitchers:

Wells, 2–0.

Cone, 4–1.

Pettitte, 4–1.

Hideki Irabu, 4–1.

Hernandez, 3–2.

But perhaps the sweetest moment for a Yankee pitcher comes for one who had not pitched for them in thirty years: Jim Bouton.

Bouton had won 20 games for the Yankees as a kid in the sixties, famous for putting so much into every pitch that his cap kept flying off his head. But that is not why he is famous in baseball. He is famous for writing Ball Four, *a funny, honest, raunchy behind-the-scenes look at life in the big leagues in the sixties. The public loved it, made it a huge best-seller that even became a sitcom eventually, with Bouton as one of the stars.*

Bouton's former teammates hated it, mostly because he had blown their covers, shown their life on the road especially as the frat-house life that it was. And is.

Bouton went on to write more books, and become a sportscaster, and even made a lot of money with bubble gum that came in a pouch like chewing tobacco. But from the time Ball Four *was published— Bouton had moved on by then, to the expansion Seattle Pilots—he had been an outcast at Yankee Stadium, never once invited to participate in Old-timer's Day.*

Until now.

His son Michael wrote the Yankees a letter about his father, in the form of a lovely Father's Day column in the Sunday New York Times, *asking that his father be invited back to Old-timer's Day, back into the Yankee family.*

Fathers and sons.

Michael Bouton is thirty-four. His sister Laurie had been killed in an automobile accident in 1996. As a brother and a son, he wrote of his father's pain. And George Steinbrenner, the Yankee owner, made sure that Jim Bouton was invited to Old-timers' Day, a month after Father's Day, 1998.

"Enough is enough," Steinbrenner said.

Bouton returns to Yankee Stadium, as a Yankee, on a Saturday in July. He dresses in the Yankee clubhouse, puts on No. 56 again, at the age of fifty-nine. He jokes with old friends and talks of making peace with Mickey Mantle—legend always had it that he was more upset about Ball Four *than anyone—before Mantle died. And he talks about the late Laurie Bouton.*

"After I got the phone call from the Yankees, I was thinking, 'Laurie's still here,'" Bouton says. *"I mean, her death led to Michael's letter, which led to the invitation. I'm not a religious man, but I'm spiritual enough to know she was involved in this."*

He walks down the tunnel toward the field eventually, is besieged by photographers and reporters when he gets to the dugout. Finally it is time to walk on the field. A Yankee at the Stadium. And now Jim Bouton does what we all do, young and old, all of us lucky to make it here, even if it is only once, the way it was only once for my dad. Bouton looks down at the grass as if seeing it this close for the very first time. He looks up and around at all the blue that seems to reach the blue of the sky.

Not a Joe DiMaggio day for him.

Maybe a Laurie Bouton day.

· *five* ·

August

D ARRYL S TRAWBERRY SAT WITH C HRIS AND A LEX
and Zach in the green room at HBO Studio Productions, on East
Twenty-third Street in Manhattan. It was a Monday morning, and he
was getting ready to tape a television interview with me for the
ESPN2 show I was doing at the time. Across the summer there had
been a lot of ballplayers, and managers, and ex-managers. David
Cone of the Yankees had been here. So had Mike Piazza, after being
traded to the Mets. And Bobby Valentine, the Mets manager, and
Tommy Lasorda, the ex–Dodgers manager. The boys would ask me
each week who the guest was going to be, decide whether they
wanted to come in for the taping and meet him.

They had been pointing toward Strawberry for a couple of weeks.

They all had bought new baseballs with allowance money for him to sign, had brought their Darryl Strawberry cards with them. Christopher brought a Yankee cap. On the ride in, they had read chapter and verse to me about Strawberry's career from the backs of the baseball cards. This was the same excited chatter that would fill the car on the way to the ballpark on a Saturday afternoon, every trip to the park like the first one, depending on which team the Yankees or Mets were playing.

All the information off these cards was presented to me as if it were a great big important exclusive.

Zach: "Did you know Darryl was Rookie of the *Year?*"

I do, I told Zach. I even saw him play that season.

"Back in 1983?"

He frowned.

"That was four years before Chris was even *born.*"

In the worldview of the two younger boys, all meaningful history of any kind began with the birth of their older brother.

"He hit thirty-nine home runs in a season and led the league," Alex said.

He sure did, I said. I thought he might be a guy who could hit 60 once, I said.

"Why didn't he?" Chris said.

I said, ask him, you're going to meet him in a few minutes.

Now they had met him. It was taking longer than usual to set up for the studio audience, because so many people had come to see Darryl. There was something about him now, because there always had been. He had always drawn a crowd, all the way back to the Little League games he and his pal Eric Davis would play back in South Central Los Angeles. Now he had drawn another to this tiny studio.

While he waited, in an elegant-looking suit, he sat and talked seriously about the Yankee season with my kids. They interviewed him and he interviewed them.

"Why are the Yankees so good?"

Zach. At six, he already knows the statistics on the backs of the cards better than his brothers.

"Because we play as a team," Darryl said. "A lot of teams I've been on, we might've had as much talent, but sometimes they worried more about themselves than winning the game."

"Is this team better than that one Mets team you played on?"

Chris.

"Yes," Darryl said. "That team won a hundred and eight games in the regular season, but I think we're gonna win more."

It went like that.

Alex took most of it in. His card was a Fleer Tradition. One of his specials. Darryl in a Yankee uniform, wearing a batting helmet, signing autographs. When Alex had gotten the card, he had worn his Yankee batting helmet in all backyard games for a week.

Darryl looked at him.

"You got any questions?"

Alex smiled and said he was fine.

"Who's your favorite Yankee?" Darryl asked him.

Alex turned around and showed him that the name on the back of his navy T-shirt was "Jeter."

"How come you like Derek?"

"He's cool," Alex said.

"You like him 'cause he's a young guy, don't you?" Darryl Strawberry said.

Alex nodded. He looked up at Strawberry and said, "Are you old?"

Now Darryl Strawberry smiled.

"I am," he said. "But my bat's still young."

ONCE, IN 1986, HE WAS ONE OF THE HOME-RUN hitters that everyone talked about in baseball. Strawberry was twenty-four and hit balls into the parking lot and the Mets won those 108 games in the regular season, then eight more in the playoffs on their way to winning the World Series. He was the slugger to watch, he was the action hero the way McGwire and Sosa were now. He was on a New York baseball team that was called one of the greatest to ever play.

He did not chase 60 home runs, because no one in baseball, not even the top guys, did at that time. But he made ballparks look impossibly small sometimes, the way McGwire and Sosa now did, and Ken Griffey, Jr. And Greg Vaughn of the Padres. And Albert Belle of the White Sox. All the sluggers of the moment.

He made the park come to a stop four times a game, or five. He had that kind of power. One of those parking-lot swings. Sometimes it was a scoreboard swing. One night against the Houston Astros, Strawberry hit a ball off the scoreboard in right center field at Shea Stadium that you swore made a sound that everybody in baseball could hear.

One that dented every single scoreboard in the whole sport.

"You think you'll only get one team like that in your life," Strawberry was saying one Sunday morning in the Yankee clubhouse, a couple of weeks before the television show. "You think you'll only get one season like that."

So he thought. By September 4, the '98 Yankees would have 100 victories. And at the age of thirty-six, even playing part-time as a designated hitter and occasional left fielder, Strawberry was still one of the team leaders in home runs. He was still averaging one ball out of the park every twelve times to the plate.

"I still got some pop in me," he said.

I wasn't the only one who thought he would break home-run records once. Everybody did. When he first got to New York with the Mets in 1983, the year before the Oakland A's signed McGwire, two years before Omar Minaya signed Sosa, it was Strawberry who was going to be the most famous home-run hitter of his time. He was Rookie of the Year for the Mets in 1983, hit 26 home runs. There was a night in San Diego when he hit two against the Padres, and Dick Williams, the Padres' manager that year, compared Darryl to the young Ted Williams. A tall, skinny kid with a long uppercut swing who could hit the ball out of sight from the start.

Before he was thirty, he would be the home-run king of the National League, he would help the Mets win the 1986 World Series, he would have 280 home runs in the big leagues. In the middle 1980s, he and his friend Dwight Gooden were two of the most exciting young stars in the game. The most exciting figures in the game have always been home-run hitters and fastball pitchers. They had talent, they had New York. One had the arm, the other had the bat. What could get in the way?

They were ahead of the field, in the clear.

Drugs and arm problems got in the way for Gooden. Everything got in the way for Darryl Strawberry. Life got in the way, mostly.

January 1990: He is arrested for pointing a .25-caliber pistol at the head of his first wife, Lisa. No charges are filed. A few days later, Strawberry checks into the Smithers treatment center on the Upper East Side of Manhattan, perhaps fifteen minutes by car from Shea Stadium. He says this is for a problem with alcohol, never telling the doctors there that he had been using cocaine throughout the 1980s, even during his glory years with the Mets.

In 1991, he signs a five-year, $20.25 million contract with the Dodgers. He hits 28 home runs that season with 99 RBIs, but then plays just 75 games the next two seasons because of a bad back.

And now his life begins to hit him the way he used to hit everybody.

In September of 1993, he is arrested for striking his then-girlfriend Charisse, whom he would later marry.

By January of 1994, the United States Attorney's office in White Plains, New York, officially begins an investigation of several members of the '86 Mets on possible tax-evasion charges. In April of that year, three days before Opening Day, Strawberry disappears from the Dodgers. He finally surfaces, though he never fully explains where he's been. It is here that he finally admits to a drug problem. This time he checks into the Betty Ford Clinic in Palm Springs. When he is released from Betty Ford, the Dodgers release Strawberry. A month later, he signs with the Giants, hits four home runs for them in the month before the players' strike in August ends the season.

In January of '95, Strawberry learns from his attorneys that the Internal Revenue Service and the U.S. Attorney's office have an airtight case against him, and that he is looking at six months of jail time at least. He has a relapse with drugs, the Giants release him. Four months later, in April, he stands in a White Plains courtroom, pleads guilty to a tax felony charge, and is sentenced by Judge Barrington Parker to six months of house arrest. Strawberry, already in a terrible financial hole because of the divorce settlement with his first wife and a full decade of excess, is forced to pay back taxes and interest totaling $350,000.

In June of that year, he becomes a New York Yankee. He gets 87 at bats over the rest of the season, hits just three home runs. The Yankees don't offer him a contract for the '96 season, and so Darryl Strawberry, at the age of thirty-four, goes to St. Paul to play for a team called the Saints in the independent Northern League. The headline writers have a wonderful time with the idea of a famous baseball sinner like Darryl finally making it to the Saints.

But George Steinbrenner, the Yankee owner, calls one more time. Steinbrenner and Bob Watson, the Yankee general manager, decide the Yankees need more pop from the left side of the plate. And no matter what, Darryl has always had that pop. He comes back to the Yankees in July and hits 11 home runs the rest of the season, then hits three home runs against the Orioles in the American League Championship Series and makes a huge catch against the Braves in the World Series. An amazing story, a crazy novel of modern sports, ends with him coming back to New York and winning another Series.

A spring training knee injury takes almost all of the '97 season from him, eventually results in surgery. Now he is back again. Clean and sober, happily married to Charisse, leading the best team in baseball in home runs for most of the summer.

"I can't change what I did," he says. "I can't change the person I was. I can only work on being the best person and best hitter I can be now. I'll never be the player I thought I would be when I was a kid. Or you thought I was going to be. Or anybody thought I was going to be. But I think I turned out all right."

He sits there in the Yankee clubhouse and talks about the old days with the Mets, and now, in the summer of '98, it is Strawberry who sends waves of memories, good and bad, careening around the place.

I had known him since he was the fresh prince of the Mets. Like the fresh prince of baseball. And he was hard to take sometimes. Once, in spring training, he had threatened to stuff me in a garbage can for something another columnist had written. Later that day, a member of the Mets' front office, Joe McIlvaine, found me on a back field in St. Petersburg, where the Mets used to train. McIlvaine apologized for the scene earlier in the clubhouse and then said, "Can I ask you a question?"

"Sure."

"Was Darryl drunk when this happened?"

"Joe, it was nine-thirty in the morning."

McIlvaine said, "Was he drunk?"

"I don't think he was."

McIlvaine thanked me and walked away, and maybe that was the first day when I looked down the road and saw everything ending badly for the home-run kid who was supposed to have it all.

Another time I interviewed him for *Esquire* magazine and he had bad things to say about just about everybody on the Mets. When the magazine came out, Strawberry denied everything. He let me down the way he would let down just about everybody in his life before he was through.

Another time, in the winter of '95 when he couldn't get a job in baseball, I interviewed him on another television show. Charles Grodin, who had a nightly show on CNBC at that time, asked me to guest-host for a couple of nights. I called Darryl in Palm Springs and told him I was going to let him do an infomercial for himself.

"What do you want me to do?" he said.

"Show everybody you're not a bum and somebody ought to give you one more chance."

"Like taking a personal ad out in the papers," he said.

"Just on TV."

He went on that night and took the blame for everything that had happened to him. At last, he sounded like a grown-up. He did the show and the phone didn't ring and he went back to working out with college kids and minor-league ballplayers in Palm Springs until the phone finally did ring and it was the Yankees calling the first time.

Through it all with Strawberry, all the way until he finally made it all the way back to the top with the Yankees, I was like everybody who had ever known him: I thought he had a good heart, and that his heart might pull him through. Yes, his friends would say, he's made a mess of his life. He's made a mess of baseball. He's thrown his prime away, and most of his money. But Darryl's got a good heart. He was one of those people you meet in sports who get into *your* heart and won't get out.

Even coming out of South Central L.A. his talent had always spoiled him. He had never been the teenager off the bus the way Sosa had, playing to an audience of one scout in an empty ballpark, trying to show enough to have a future. People had always come to watch Darryl Strawberry. He would go deep again for Crenshaw High School, or in the minors, and the only question was just how big a future he would have, how far into the record books his home runs would land.

Then he had to end up a broke, nearly busted felon before he would catch up with the last few innings of that future.

He came back. He was cheered in New York not just because of the young exciting star he had been, but because he had gotten up. He had come back again and again. He had kept getting up. Drugs and liquor and women. Blown fortunes. Bad knees. All of it. He still had that pop. Between July 13 and August 7, Strawberry had hit 10 home runs, giving him 21 for the season. If the Yankees weren't so deep with talent, if he had gotten more at bats, there's no telling how many home runs he would have hit for them. For those two weeks in July and August, he went deep again, went deep the way McGwire and Sosa had all season.

Strawberry hit them the way he had when he was young, when everybody talked about him.

"My knees are old," he said on this day.

Then he grinned, the fresh prince still, and said what he would say to my sons.

"But my bat's still young," he said.

He was sitting on a stool in front of his locker, wearing a navy T-shirt one of his teammates, Chili Davis, had given him. On the back it read, "Don't Send No Boys." Strawberry the thirty-six-year-old man sitting here on this morning talking about the boy he had been. The sleeves of the shirt had been cut off at the shoulders, showing you his massive forearms. He had always been so proud of them when he was young. Look at these dawgs, he would say. Now he just crossed those arms and smiled.

"But this is the happiest I've ever been in my life," he said. "This is the happiest I've ever been in my career. How can you not be happy, playing on a ballclub like this?"

Strawberry looked around the room. Paul O'Neill, in the back. David Cone, his old teammate with the Mets, straight across. David Wells, one locker down from Cone. Derek Jeter, the young shortstop with one World Series in the books already, trying to win his second in just three years in the major leagues. The kid on this team. Cool kid that all boys like my boys wanted to be. The Yankees had started out 1–3 the first week of the season, and we in New York were all writing that they better win some games fast or Joe Torre, the manager, might be in trouble with Steinbrenner, who had spent the past twenty-five years firing managers for sport, even managers as popular as Torre.

Since then it seemed the Yankees had won almost every day. They seemed to be ahead in every game. They won series after series, week after week. They had put themselves on a pace to win more games than any baseball team had ever won.

In New York, the Yankees were the story of the season, not home runs.

I asked Strawberry if he'd ever seen a team like this.

"No one has," he said.

He got up then, headed for the trainer's room. He said something about feeling like he must've pulled something in his stomach. Or maybe it was cramps. Later, I'd remember him joking about the cramps. But then saying it was nothing.

"This is the end of the rainbow for me," he said. "I finally put all the bad parts behind me."

What bad parts could there be for him in a season like this?

He was like his team.

In the clear.

Once he symbolized everything that was wrong with baseball, all the arrogance and excesses and selfishness of the modern athlete, all the ones who had been blessed with this kind of talent, gifts like these, and then tried to throw it all away with both hands. But now it was as if the magic of the season had touched Darryl Strawberry, too. Now he was with the Yankees, who had become as much an example as anything about how right things were with baseball.

What could possibly go wrong for him now?

It was the night of August 17 and it seemed as if the whole country was in front of television sets a little after 9 P.M., Eastern time. This was the moment we had been waiting for all summer, or so we thought. We had been conditioned to think that way by newspapers and televisions, day after day for months. There had been this almost insane buildup and hype.

Finally the guy was stepping to the plate.

Not McGwire, trying to be the first guy ever get to 50 home runs before September 1.

Not Sosa, getting a little closer to McGwire.

President Bill Clinton, finally coming clean about Monica Lewinsky.

Welcome to the show.

That afternoon, Clinton had given his taped deposition about his relationship with former White House intern Monica Lewinsky. Now he would address the country, from the White House, from the same room where he had testified before independent counsel Kenneth Starr. This was before Starr would release Clinton's testimony in September. So Americans waited to hear the President's version of what he had said that afternoon.

It had been seven months since Lewinsky's name had first surfaced; it had actually happened the weekend John Elway and the Denver Broncos had upset the Green Bay Packers in the Super Bowl. And for all of those seven months, Clinton had denied that he had engaged in a sexual relationship with Lewinsky. He had denied it and had deployed his spin troops from the White House to deny it all over Cable America every single night.

Denied it all the way to August 17.

On national television, in an extraordinary scene, the President of the United States looked into the camera and admitted that he had been involved in an inappropriate physical relationship with Monica Lewinsky. Admitted that he had lied to the country and to his family and all the aides who had defended him with such passion for seven months. But Clinton was far from contrite. He never apologized. Never said "I'm sorry" to the country. Instead, about halfway through his address, he veered away from contrition and attacked Starr for wasting millions of tax dollars on his investigation into the Clintons' finances, and into Bill Clinton's private life.

"Even presidents make mistakes," the President said.

Then he was gone and the preseason *Monday Night Football* game between the Cowboys and Patriots was back on ABC, and people were glad to have even a meaningless football game, because now the country, in some crucial way, was officially sick of this whole story, sick of Clinton, sick of Starr, sick of Starr stalking Clinton the way Captain Ahab had stalked Moby Dick, sick of a president lying this way to a grand jury and to everyone.

What once seemed racy—what did they do? where did they do

it? who saw?—and shocking now seemed as grotesque as some sort of high-class stag film.

Up to now, the baseball season had been a pleasant and occasionally glorious diversion from what was happening in Washington, D.C., the numbing regularity of the scandals, small shabby details being added day by day, like some form of cable-television torture. We could always leave Bill-and-Monica for Mark-and-Sammy. But something changed the week of August 17. Bill-and-Monica wasn't going anywhere, of course, and there was still the shabby release of Clinton's testimony and all the impeachment talk, at least until the November elections, when the voters ended all that by telling all candidates that they were retiring Monica Lewinsky from public life.

Suddenly, baseball was more than a diversion. Suddenly, it seemed like a cure. Every day there was this corner of American life where we could go to escape from Lawyers on Television, from nightly news we were constantly softening and explaining to our children. There was this place of triumph, involving the most basic action in sports: the home-run swing. It required no complicated analysis or explanation. Even the most casual fan could follow it the way they could some old-fashioned movie serial. It was all there for us, every day, in the papers, on the television: how many home runs they had, how many games there were left to play, where they stood against the standards Ruth and Maris had set once.

No phone polls needed to decide how we felt about all this, no talking hairdos on television telling us how we were supposed to feel. We knew how we felt. We felt great. This was a sports story pure and good out of another time, one not choked with money or greed or sex or the kind of crime stories that seemed to dominate the culture of sports in the country more and more.

All the country wanted to know was what my sons wanted to know when they woke in the morning, checked the notes on the floor.

Did McGwire hit another?

Did Sosa?

They became the couple we wanted to see, and know about, and talk about. The night after Clinton's address, McGwire's Cardinals went to Wrigley Field to play Sosa's Cubs.

They were the main event now. Baseball was the main event. After the peep show of Bill-and-Monica, baseball suddenly became the compelling theater of the country. Somehow, after all the months of Bill-and-Monica, president and intern, we wanted to talk about something else. We wanted the conversation to be about something that made us feel good. We wanted to talk baseball. McGwire and Sosa weren't just going to knock the cover off the ball now. For six grand weeks in the country, all over the country, they were about to knock sex off the front page.

For the end of this one summer, maybe the old cliché was true, maybe you could understand America a little better by understanding baseball. We were tired of being locked inside that study next to the Oval Office; we wanted to be outside, in fresh air, on green grass, watching new baseball heroes challenge heroes from the past, challenge the most important record in all of sports.

Welcome to the real show.

THE WEATHER IN CHICAGO WAS SPLENDID, MORE early autumn than late summer. A gentle wind, temperature in the sixties. McGwire and Sosa were tied at 47 home runs by now. Neither hit a home run in Tuesday night's game. But in a season when everything seemed to break right, when everything kept falling into place, maybe they were just looking for one of the most perfect baseball settings imaginable: Wrigley Field in the afternoon, Wrigley under blue skies, with an air show over Lake Michigan and vintage airplanes buzzing the ballpark all day long.

Classic planes, classic baseball.

As always, the fans waited out on Waveland Avenue and in the Wrigley bleachers, one of the sweet, raucous, wonderful neighborhoods in all of sports, now or ever. In the bleachers that day, a fan sitting in a beach chair was asked what he would do if Sosa was the one to hit No. 62 first, and did it here.

"If it was hit out here," the man said, "I wouldn't chase it. But if it rolled right up to me, I would certainly pick it up."

Baseball at Wrigley in the afternoon. You could imagine Ruth in this place when Ruth was the home-run king and calling his shot against the Cubs, or so legend always had it, in the 1932 World Series. On this afternoon, there were all the other places in baseball and there was this place, because now the home runs had come here, both McGwire and Sosa were tied and they were here, and wasn't this the way it was all supposed to look?

Wasn't this the way sports was supposed to make you feel?

In the bottom of the fifth inning, with Kent Bottenfield pitching for the Cardinals, Sammy Sosa homered into the left-field stands to put the Cubs ahead 6–2. He had taken the home-run lead away from McGwire. It was 48–47 at Wrigley. There were 39,689 in attendance and some of them were Cardinals fans, because Cubs–Cardinals had been a rivalry long before McGwire–Sosa was. The Cubs fans chanted Sosa's name and sat down finally, but then were back up when he came out to right field in the top of the sixth.

In the bottom of the seventh Sosa walked, and when he got to first base and stood next to McGwire, McGwire smiled and imitated the finger-kissing that had become Sosa's signature gesture after another home run. And even as big and muscular as Sosa had become as an adult, when you saw him standing there, laughing with McGwire, looking so much smaller than McGwire, you could see the charming boy in him.

The boy in both of them.

They stood there and laughed with each other and people would wonder later what they were talking about, and it turned out they were talking about opening a golf course together in Sosa's country, the Dominican Republic.

"What do you suppose we should call it?" McGwire asked.

" 'The Home Run Trap,' " Sosa said.

They laughed a little more at Wrigley, a couple of kids with time to kill on a summer day, as if the world weren't watching, as if they had all the time in the world, even though there were just six weeks left in the season.

By the time McGwire came to the plate in the top of the eighth, he had gone his last twenty at bats without a home run, going all the way back to August 11. The Cardinals had cut the Cubs' lead to 6–5 by then. There was one out when McGwire hit a Matt Karchner pitch out of Wrigley Field and all the way out to Waveland Avenue. He had tied the game and he had tied Sosa.

Forty-eight all.

Two innings later, Mark McGwire hit a Terry Mulholland fastball so high and deep to center that you worried about the vintage airplanes. The Cardinals were ahead 7–6, on their way to an 8–6 victory, and now McGwire was back in the home-run lead. Afterward they asked McGwire about the week-long slump, and he said, "It's just a matter of getting balls to hit. And today I got two balls to hit, that's really all about it."

But he was back in a groove now. How Mark got his groove back. He would never really seem to lose it the rest of the way. And something else would happen the rest of the way: McGwire himself would begin to enjoy his own show. Maybe it was the sight of Sosa on the same field, reveling in it all, that helped him along. Maybe enough people told him behind the scenes that he would be remembered as much for the way he handled the stage as for the home runs; that poor Roger Maris, a good man, was forever marked surly for the way he dealt with the media and attention in '61. There had been a day earlier in August, when it seemed McGwire had begun to fade a bit, that McGwire was asked by ESPN if he thought his swing might need a little work.

"Don't worry about my swing," McGwire snapped. "Worry about your families."

Maris in '61 all over again.

McGwire looked tired and he looked testy in the part of the season that had always been known as the dog days of August. Big old whipped ornery dog on this day.

"That's what you guys are going to use tonight, isn't it?" he said.

Meaning the "Worry about your families" sound bite.

The answer was obviously yes. And for a week or so, people wondered if McGwire was another slugger who was cracking the closer he got to Maris's record. There was talk around the batting cage about a temporary hitch in McGwire's swing. In the end, the early part of August was the temporary hitch. McGwire started to hit again. He made the trip to Wrigley, right before he got a hero's welcome at Shea Stadium in New York.

This was the week of the season when Mark McGwire allowed himself to smile, when the big man let the little boy out for good. At first base at Wrigley, standing next to the beaming Sosa, and everywhere else.

As a child in San Pedro de Macoris, Sosa had helped support his family by shining shoes and selling fruit on the street.

"That's pressure," he said. "This is just baseball."

But such wonderful baseball.

Back in 1997, the Cubs had been severely criticized throughout baseball for giving Sammy Sosa a four-year, $42.5 million contract. You heard that Sosa was just another wild swinger who would get even wilder now that he was into the big money. He was undisciplined and would only get worse. And everyone who said this or screamed it on the radio was wrong. Somehow the contract seemed to make Sosa more determined, more focused, more set on finding how much greatness he might have in him. And more relaxed. This was the teenaged boy off the bus, still burning to show everybody, not just one scout, how much ball he had in him. Sometimes the money ruins the player, and sometimes the player decides to earn it.

Sosa moved into the same high-rise apartment building where Oprah Winfrey lived in Chicago. There was enough room in it for his whole family to visit. And maybe McGwire's too. The Rangers had traded Sosa away for a veteran hitter named Harold Baines. The White Sox had traded him away, and before they did, Sosa heard that he wore too much jewelry and swung much too hard. Finally, Sosa felt he had found a home. In Chicago. At Wrigley Field.

After the Wednesday-afternoon game in Chicago, McGwire said, "Even though I'm on the other side and we're playing against him and I want to see our team win, it's just awesome to see that kind of talent and the way Sammy goes about his business."

Sosa smiled and blew another kiss.

"Mark is the man," he said, only because he had said it all along, had made sure even after his incredible month of June that he was the supporting actor here, not the star. "Mark is the one who will break the record."

McGwire came to New York and played the Mets in a double-header at Shea Stadium and the New York crowd cheered him, embraced him every time up. He had brought the home-run summer to them now. He had brought it, for a couple of days, to Broadway. The New Yorkers at Shea knew this was it, this was their shot at McGwire, that he and the Cardinals would not be back for the rest of the season, and so they told him, in the loudest possible way, what they thought about what he was doing, what Sosa was doing, how the whole sport was doing. It was a celebration of home runs and of the game.

And McGwire delivered.

On August 20, in the first game of a doubleheader, McGwire became the first man in major-league history to hit 50 home runs in three consecutive seasons. Ruth had never done it. No one had. Until now. Until McGwire got there in New York. In the first inning of the second game, McGwire hit No. 51. He exulted as he made his way around first base. All along, since the spring, he had said that the only way to have a realistic shot at Maris was to have 50 by September.

"That's what I truly believe," McGwire had said. "Ever since I was a kid hitting home runs . . . I mean, if someone gets to fifty by September 1, they have a shot down the stretch run."

On this day, another historic day in the summer of '98, McGwire had also become the oldest player to ever hit 50 in a season. He was thirty-four years and 324 days, a month and change away from turning thirty-five. But he acted like the kid he had been for the Oakland A's, when he first came rushing onto the stage, hitting those 49 home runs as a rookie. He seemed quite proud in New York, especially proud of having hit the 50 home runs for three straight seasons, a record that had begun with Oakland in the American League and now had traveled with him to St. Louis and the National League, showing that no league could hold McGwire. He sat there after the game and talked with excitement about the work he had done and the work still left for him to do, and it was as if he was still carried along by the cheers, the way New York had sounded for him.

Mark McGwire, who had started all this back in April, who had made us care and made us watch from the very beginning, had finally joined the crowd.

The morning after McGwire hits Nos. 50 and 51, the editorial page of the *Bergen* (New Jersey) *Record* had this to say:

"For Americans, this year may be remembered for the [Lewinsky] dress, the [Clinton] confession, and the chase. We probably know more than we want to about the first two. But with Labor Day fast approaching, the pursuit of Maris's home-run mark has really heated up. The boys of summer have given us a most welcome diversion."

McGwire touched home plate at Shea Stadium and turned for home. We all cheered him on. We all watched him go. Once there had been the song "Mrs. Robinson" from Paul Simon in the 1960s, with perhaps Simon's most famous line:

"Where have you gone, Joe DiMaggio?
A nation turns its lonely eyes to you. . . ."

In a different time, in a different America, the America of Monica's dress and a president's lies, the nation's eyes turned toward McGwire and Sosa.

In August . . .

After the game of August 31, somehow, impossibly, McGwire and Sosa are tied with 55 home runs.

Somehow a baseball team, the Yankees, had nearly gotten to 100 victories by September 1; their record through August 31 was 98–37.

By now, the Yankees were 18 games ahead of the Red Sox and the most intriguing race in baseball, even with a close race between the Texas Rangers and the Anaheim Angels in the American League West, was the one for the wild card in the National League. With a month to go, Mike Piazza's Mets were tied with Sosa's Cubs, both teams having records of 76–62.

Two games behind were the Giants, led by Barry Bonds, only the greatest player of his time in baseball.

"Oh, I'm just off to the side now," he is saying one afternoon in the visitors' clubhouse at Shea Stadium before the Giants play the Mets. "First Junior [Griffey] was the golden child. Now you've got McGwire and Sosa. I'm just an old man trying to keep up, best I can."

Then he laughs. And jokes on this day about the treatment Piazza has received from Mets fans across his first couple of months in New York. Piazza has not hit with runners in scoring position and has gotten booed for that, and killed on WFAN, the sports-talk station in New York. The Yankees are clearly a team for the ages and make everybody in New York happy all the time. So Piazza becomes a whipping boy, at least until he gets hot in September and everybody loves him to death.

"He's getting booed?" Bonds shouts. "They're killing him on the radio? Well, welcome to my whole damn career."

He shakes his head.

"Man, I was made for this town," he says. "Can you imagine what it would have been like? Headlines every day, like they had when Reggie [Jackson] was here. I love it here. You want to know why? Because if the fans give it to me, I give it right back."

He is the only player in baseball history to have 400 home runs and 400 stolen bases. He has always been a superb outfielder. He was MVP of the National League three times. The son of Bobby Bonds, godson of Willie Mays, he is the best all-around player, in every single facet of baseball, since Mays. And after a terrible slump early in the season, he is coming on hard now, finishing the way he always does, ready to carry the Giants again in September, all the way to a playoff with Sosa's Cubs for the wild card, which the Giants will lose in Wrigley Field.

In what must feel like an off year to him, he will end up with 37 homers, 122 RBIs, a batting average of .303, 28 stolen bases.

The night before, the fans at Shea toss coins at him in the outfield, the way they have for years. Bonds laughs, puts the money in his pocket. Late in the game, he yells over at Giants center fielder Ellis Burks.

"If anybody hits one in the alley," Barry Bonds says to Burks, "you gotta get it. My pockets are too loaded down with money."

He laughs again. He says he is an old man, but is younger than McGwire, having just turned thirty-four at the end of July. He talks about the others being golden children, and still plays like one himself. Small change in his pockets, but a whole career that seems to be made of gold. . . .

six

September

(first half)

CHRISTOPHER SAID, "HAS ANYBODY EVER PITCHED two perfect games in the same season?"

We were in my study, watching the Yankees play the Oakland A's at the Stadium. It was the bottom of the fourth, David Wells pitching against Tom Candiotti, an ancient knuckleballer. So far for the A's, it had been nine batters up and nine down.

"No one has ever pitched two perfect games, period," I said. "A guy named Johnny Vander Meer once pitched two straight no-hitters for the Reds back in the thirties. Allie Reynolds, an old Yankee pitcher, pitched two no-hitters in 1951. But nobody has ever pitched two perfect games in the same season."

"What if Wells does?"

"It's only the third inning."

"Jim Kaat just said he's got better stuff than he did against the Twins."

Meaning the perfect game against the Twins in May. Kaat, a great left-hander of the sixties and seventies and eighties, won 283 games in the big leagues, and was now a Yankee television analyst on the Madison Square Garden network.

I went to put the younger boys to bed, and by the time I came back, Wells was through the fourth.

Twelve A's up now, twelve down.

I went upstairs and grabbed a blazer out of my closet, came running down the steps. Taylor, my wife, looked at me.

"It's nearly nine o'clock. Where are you going?"

"Back to the Stadium."

Our home in Connecticut is about forty-five minutes from the Bronx, without traffic. The Merritt Parkway to the Hutchinson Parkway to the Cross County Expressway to the Major Deegan Expressway. You see the signs for the George Washington Bridge and then you come around a big curve and then, before you know it, like the first level of stars in the night, there are the lights to the Stadium.

"You just got back from the Stadium a little while ago."

"I know."

Taylor said, "I don't suppose there's any reason to ask why."

"Wells might pitch another perfect game. I have to see at least some of it if he does. Nothing like this has ever happened before."

"You've said that all season."

I had said that all season, and now, the ball in Wells's left hand again, all the mystery and snap back in his breaking ball, I was saying it again. The Yankees had come into this game against the A's with a record of 98–37. They were now 18 games ahead of the second-place Red Sox in the American League East. The A's were tied for last place in the American League West. There should have been nothing special about the first night of September.

Except you couldn't miss a night with the Yankees.

You couldn't miss a night with them the way you couldn't miss a swing of McGwire's, or Sosa's.

They might give you another one of those memories that would never stop rolling as long as you lived.

I HAD GONE TO THE BALLPARK EARLIER IN THE DAY because the Yankees were honoring the Little League champs from Toms River. The kids and the coaches and the parents would come up the New Jersey Turnpike by bus and the kids would meet the Yankees before the game. Right before the game started, they would all be out on the field with the Yankees, position by position. The Toms River right fielder would stand with O'Neill in right. The shortstop, Todd Frazier, would be out at short with Jeter. Casey Gaynor, the starting pitcher, would stand on the pitcher's mound at the Stadium with Wells.

Of all the ceremonies since they'd beaten Japan, of all the sights, what could be better than these sights, this view of the Stadium? My dad found out that day in August three years before, when he finally made it out on that grass. Now these kids would do the same. They all want to make it out of the stands, make it out on that field, and play for the Yankees. When Jeter was young, his grandmother from New Jersey used to bring him up the Turnpike sometimes for Sunday-afternoon games. Now he was the Yankee shortstop, playing where he had seen Bucky Dent play.

On this night, the Toms River kids would walk the blue line the Yankees walked, all the way to the field at the Stadium.

The bus pulled up a little before seven, and the photographers and the television cameras were waiting for it outside, and before long the kids were in front of the Yankee dugout, posing for pictures with the Yankees as the Yankees warmed up for the A's, giving interviews, trying to get autographed balls and bats off both the Yankees and the A's, laughing and poking each other and pointing at every corner of the place at once.

Kids their own age were leaning over the Yankee dugout, begging the Little Leaguers for autographs at the same time they were asking the Yankees for the same thing.

Kids reaching out to other kids who were a little closer to the action, a little closer to the season.

Frazier or Gaynor, wearing their black jerseys, would walk over, cool as pros, and catch the balls, catch the pens the kids would throw, sign their names—very professionally—and throw the balls back.

As they did, though, they kept looking behind them, to make sure they weren't missing any of the action behind them. Just because they didn't want to miss anything on this night, either.

"How does it look?" Todd Frazier was asked.

He grinned and said it looked exactly the way it was supposed to look.

"It looks very, very cool," he said.

"Bigger than you thought it would be from inside?"

"Oh yeah," he said. "Much, *much* bigger."

Then his head whipped around, some kind of radar that boys his age seem to have—somebody getting stuff—and saw Jason Giambi of the A's walking toward the Toms River team, with a bat he had broken in batting practice.

"Who wants it?" Giambi said.

And nearly got trampled by the Little League champions of the whole world, because they all wanted that bat bad. They wanted to own that bat, Giambi's bat, put it in the shrine of their own stuff, the way my kids would have wanted it. They ran for Giambi the way Alex's Ontarios would have.

Then they went out and stood with the Yankees.

"How you feelin'?" Wells said to Casey Gaynor on the mound.

"Great!" Gaynor said.

Wells laughed.

As always, Wells was the biggest kid in the place.

"The reason I'm asking," Wells said, "is because you might have to come in for me tonight."

Gaynor, pitcher to pitcher, told Wells he was ready.

The kids came off the field, one more cheer for them in their summer of cheers, the game started, and Wells slapped the A's around in the top of the first. I thought I had seen the sweetest and best part of the night, got into the car, put the game on the radio, listened to John Sterling and Michael Kay on WABC, put the lights of the Stadium behind me, and headed up the Deegan.

It turned out Wells didn't need any help from Casey Gaynor.

I DROVE FAST, HOPING THE YANKEES WOULD HAVE at least one big inning. They had been giving us big innings all season; now all I needed was one more. When they scored runs they seemed to score them in bunches, and half an inning could take half an hour. One of those and I was in the clear, provided Wells kept getting everybody out. On the radio, I could hear the roar of the crowd at two strikes, picture everybody in the place getting up, calling for a strikeout. The catcher was Jorge Posada, who had caught Wells's perfect game on May 17.

I called my dad from the car phone between the bottom of the fifth and the top of the sixth.

"Guess where I'm going?" and I told him where, and why.

"You're getting too old for this, son," he said.

"Not always."

The game wasn't on television in New Hampshire, but he said he could get the Yankees on the radio sometimes.

"Seven-seventy on the dial," I said.

"I know," he said.

The paid attendance that night was 29,000. In all, there were 36,000 in the ballpark. They sounded like 56,000, a full house, as Wells got through the sixth inning. On the radio, you could hear the excitement building in both Sterling and Kay, the way it had back in May, when Christopher and I had listened in this same car.

"Call your friends," Michael Kay said. "Call anybody you can think of and tell them to put on the television or put on the radio, because David Wells has another perfect game going at the Stadium."

Through the fifth, through the sixth.

I was on the Cross County by now, maybe ten minutes from the ballpark, maybe a little more.

Joe Torre had replaced Tim Raines, his starting left fielder, in the sixth inning, bringing in Chad Curtis, a better fielder than Raines, one with younger legs. Torre said he did it hoping that Wells wouldn't notice, wouldn't think his manager—even trying to help—had done something to jinx him. Wells noticed, of course. He notices everything. When he saw Curtis in left, he turned on the mound and glared into the Yankee dugout at Torre, who looked away so the pitcher known as Boomer wouldn't see him stifling a laugh.

"I was thinking, 'Dear God, please don't let anything happen in this inning,'" Torre would say later. "And it didn't. Boomer may have been relieved when he made it through the sixth with the thing intact. But not nearly as relieved as I was."

The seventh now.

Nine outs away.

Wells went to 3–0 on Rickey Henderson. Once, when Henderson was young, the late great sports columnist Jim Murray had described Henderson's strike zone as being smaller than Hitler's soul. Henderson hadn't grown, and neither had his strike zone.

Wells came back and got Henderson to line to O'Neill in right field.

Eight outs away.

I was on the Deegan, driving way too fast, coming around the curve. Seeing those lights, hearing the cheers on the radio. Or maybe they were the real cheers now.

Two outs in the seventh, seven outs to go, Jason Giambi at the plate.

Giambi, who had one less good bat than he'd started the night with, because he'd given one away to the champs from Toms River.

He singled past Chuck Knoblauch into center field as I pulled into the parking lot at Yankee Stadium, and Wells's second perfect game was gone. I jumped out of the car, and as soon as I did, I could hear the end of the ovation that had begun on the radio.

I ran past Darryl Knowling, who presides over the players' parking lot the way a great maître d' presides over a restaurant, and he was smiling, shaking his head, looking up himself now at the Stadium lights, the noise that seemed to rise out of them now like high Wells heat.

"Has this season been a kick in the ass or what?" Knowling said.

In the clubhouse afterward, Wells—who would end up allowing one more hit after Giambi's—seemed almost relieved that more history for him had just eluded Knoblauch's glove. He sat with a huge icepack attached to his left shoulder and a bottle of water in his hand, though you knew something else, stronger, would be in that hand soon. The end of the game was just the beginning of the night sometimes for David Wells.

"I said to David Cone, 'I can't believe this is happening again,' " Wells said.

On the floor behind him, leaning against a wall of his locker, was an old front page from the New York *Daily Mirror*, the day after Don Larsen's perfect game in 1956. Behind Wells, in the manager's office, Torre said, "If you can do it once, you can do it again."

In a crazy season, a wonderful season, when all things were possible for home-run hitters and Joe Torre's baseball team, when a balding tattooed pitcher who liked motorcycles and beer and Babe Ruth, tried to be perfect again.

When that crazy pitcher showed some Little Leaguers how the big guys do it.

I WROTE A COLUMN FOR THE *DAILY NEWS* ABOUT David Wells and drove home for good.

Everybody in the house was sleeping.

My wife had left *me* a note, reminding me that the boys wanted notes, as if I needed reminding. I sat down at the kitchen table and wrote three more columns, my last of the night, very short columns, for three sleeping boys, the oldest of whom went to bed dreaming that Wells still had a chance.

Wells was seven outs away.
Jason Giambi got a hit in the 7th.
It ended up a three-hitter.
Yanks won.

AT THE END OF CHRISTOPHER'S, I ADDED THIS:

I wish I could have taken you with me, pal.
It wasn't as much fun listening in the car without you.
Love, Dad.

It was only a matter of time now in Fargo, North Dakota, which was still Maris country, even if he had moved away long ago, lived out the last years of his life in Florida. Fargo still considered itself Roger Maris's home. There was a modest Roger Maris museum in a downtown shopping mall. There was still the annual Roger Maris golf tournament, benefiting a local hospice, attracting so many old Yankees, other baseball celebrities.

Fargo would always be the capital of Maris.

But even in Fargo, they were prepared to let go now that McGwire had gotten to 60 homers on the Saturday of Labor Day Weekend. They had been preparing in Fargo all summer.

"We had our turn for thirty-seven years," Don Gooselaw said on Sunday morning. "Now it's somebody else's turn."

He had been a Maris guy his whole life, as long as he could remember. Gooselaw knew Roger Maris long before the country knew, long before he was MVP of the American League in 1960, long before he hit 61 home runs and made Fargo the capital of home runs, too. They had grown up together in Grand Forks, in the Hampton Apartments on Fifth Avenue and Seventh Street. This was the beginning of a friendship that would last all of Maris's life, until he finally died of leukemia in 1985, at the age of fifty-one.

Boyhood memories of Maris, much closer to home than my own.

"I was as close to baseball history as you could get, I suppose," Gooselaw said. "I used to go to Minneapolis when the Yankees would play there. I was with Roger in Cincinnati for the World Series in '61. The home-run year. I thought of him as my best friend. But even here in North Dakota, you have to let go eventually."

Maris's family had moved to Fargo in the forties after Roger's fa-

ther, a railroad man, had been transferred out of Grand Forks.
Gooselaw stayed behind in Fargo. When Maris would come back to
town in his retirement, the two of them would reminisce about playing high school football against each other, Gooselaw as a quarterback for St. James High and Maris as a halfback for Shanley. They
would make themselves bigger and faster than they had been, make
the games they'd played even more dramatic than they were, argue
about which team was really better.

"You could get Roger to brag on football, once he got going,"
Gooselaw said. "Never baseball."

He was asked if Maris ever talked much about 1961, when he was
McGwire and Mickey Mantle was Sosa, and everybody watched
them, everybody talked about them.

"Not unless you asked him," Gooselaw said. "Roger never
brought it up himself. I sometimes got the idea that it was a happier
memory for the rest of us than it was for him."

Don Gooselaw said to me, "How old were you that year?"

I told him I was nine.

"Anything happen since that even comes close to it?"

I said, not until now.

"Even now," he said, "I have to tell you I liked '61 better. Maybe
it's because I was looking at it from here."

He was sixty-six on this day, divorced, living in an apartment a
few blocks from where the Maris family had lived after they moved
to town. He told a story about the end of the '61 season, how anxious
Maris was to get to the airport in Cincinnati and get home to Kansas
City, where the family was still living that year. Gooselaw talked
about the golf tournament, and how they'd changed the charities it
benefited over time, and how this year the money went to a local
hospice. He talked about Pat Maris, Roger's widow, and the Maris
children, how happy he was that Major League Baseball had made

sure they would be in the ballpark if McGwire broke the record in St. Louis over the next few days.

How all this time after 1961, the Maris children were able to share in what their father had done that season, even as they prepared to let go of the record, same as Fargo did.

"Everybody who ever knew their old man has had a pretty good run with this thing," Don Gooselaw said. "If McGwire breaks it today, God bless him. If he doesn't, I'll be like everybody else these next two days, watching that showdown between him and Sammy Sosa when the Cubs go in there to St. Louis. It'll be like one of those old home-run derbies they used to have on television when Roger was playing. Hell, even I know it's a once-in-a-lifetime thing those two guys have going."

His best friend, all the way back to the Hampton Apartments, came out of North Dakota and broke into the big leagues with Cleveland and got traded to Kansas City and then the Yankees, and then in his second season there broke Ruth's record. And over time, they allowed themselves to think Roger Maris's record might stand forever, that maybe McGwire and Ken Griffey, Jr., had made the best run they were going to make the year before, when McGwire had hit his 58 and Griffey had 55. That the pitchers would always get them, or the pressure.

Somehow Fargo would remain the capital of Maris and home runs.

"You get spoiled," Gooselaw said. "You take it for granted after a while. You'd see guys take their shot, get to fifty, and they'd start up talking about Roger and his pace in '61 and all that. Then they wouldn't make it and you'd think, 'Well, old Rog is still safe.' "

Maris was no longer safe. It was only a matter of time now. They knew it in Fargo as well as they knew it anywhere in America on the day before Labor Day, 1998. Maris's run, Fargo's run, would end today or tomorrow, or sometime this week, and that would be that. Don Gooselaw, who went all the way back, would watch McGwire and Sosa on the same ballfield together, playing their home-run derby, the most spectacular the game had ever seen, bigger and more colorful than what Maris and Mantle had given us.

Everywhere else, the country would choose up sides the rest of the way, rooting for McGwire or rooting for Sosa, wondering if Sosa could catch him again, or whether this would be the time in the season when McGwire pulled away for good. Everywhere else, they rooted for the balls to keep flying out of the park all the way to the last Sunday in September.

Just not here in Fargo.

Just not in Maris country, where they had been stuck on 61 since '61.

IT SEEMED AS IF THERE WAS AN HISTORIC SWING almost every day now, the history changing that fast with McGwire. Catch Ruth on Saturday. Catch Maris on Monday afternoon. But the swings themselves all looked the same. The massive arms, the ones he didn't have on Alex's rookie card, would come through and the left leg would seem to buckle as if someone had slugged McGwire from behind with a two-by-four, and the right hand would come off the bat, and then another ball would be gone, over the left-field wall usually, and McGwire would be on his way around the bases, to another standing ovation.

For No. 61, McGwire's son Matt was waiting for him at home plate, and now the father gathered up the boy, ten, in those massive arms.

Better than anyone watching the scene, the two of them would remember where they were for No. 61, exactly where they were.

"That's the thing people always want to tell you," Bobby Thom-

son said that morning at his home in New Jersey, a town called Wach-
tung. "They want to tell you where they were when you hit it."

Babe Ruth was no longer safe from McGwire, Maris was no
longer safe. Fargo was not safe. Bobby Thomson was safe. So was his
swing from October 3 in 1951, when he had hit a three-run homer off
Ralph Branca and the Brooklyn Dodgers in the bottom of the ninth
at the Polo Grounds, and Thomson's New York Giants won the third
game of a three-game playoff for the National League pennant.
Nearly half a century later, even with everything that McGwire was
doing, it was still called the single most famous home-run swing in
baseball history.

Still remembered in baseball legend—even immortalized fur-
ther by Don DeLillo in his novel *Underworld*—as "The Shot Heard
'Round the World."

There were some deep parts of baseball history that even
McGwire could not reach.

On ESPN's broadcast of McGwire's 61st, Joe Morgan had said,
"McGwire is the only man alive who knows what this feels like."
And it reminded you of the famous story about Joe DiMaggio and
Marilyn Monroe, and how she came back after entertaining the troops
in Korea and said to her then-husband, "Joe, you never heard such
cheering."

And DiMaggio said, "Yes, I have."

The circumstances were completely different for Thomson in
'51. He was not a famous slugger. He was not famous at all before
October 3 that year. Just afterward. As well as any man alive, he
knew these moments for McGwire. He knew that one moment, one
ball over the fence, could change your life, make you a baseball immortal.

"You know what the amazing thing for me is when I look at a
guy McGwire's size?" Thomson said on this day. "I was just a little
guy."

Thomson chuckled and said, "If I stood next to him, I'd look like some old guy they let be batboy."

He would turn seventy-five in October of '98, a few weeks after the anniversary of his home run against Branca. On this morning, he was on his way to his health club. Thomson was retired from a long-time job as a salesman for a Chicago-based packaging company called Stone Containers. But he still made personal appearances, so many of them with Branca, at card shows and award dinners. Over time, Thomson and Branca had become friends, even worked up a little act they did, one that included a song parody.

"Because of you," Thomson would begin, "there's a song in my heart . . ."

And Thomson, an avid golfer, still played a lot of charity golf. He had also become a spokesman for the Arthritis Foundation of New Jersey. The home run had not supported him all these years. As soon as his playing career was over he had gone to work, and until his retirement from Stone Containers, he had worked ever since. He knew that in a different sports culture, in a different time, that one swing could have made him millions. He just laughed off that kind of talk, the way he always had.

"Your career is your career," Bobby Thomson said. "Your life is your life. That home run just made mine a little happier."

I asked him on this day, with the focus of the country on Busch Stadium in St. Louis, if he found himself rooting for McGwire or for Sosa to ultimately end up with the single-season record.

"If I root for anybody, I kind of root for the Cubs, because I played for them once," Thomson said. "Mostly I've been rooting for baseball. In my heart, I always knew it would come back."

Then once more, Thomson was talking about his day in the sun, his swing, his bright forever moment, the one that gave him a happier life, the one that would always have his name up in lights, no matter how many McGwire and Sosa hit. No matter what anybody else did in baseball. There had been other dramatic postseason home runs since. Bill Mazeroski had ended Game 7 of the 1960 World Series for the Pirates with the home run that beat the Yankees. Bucky Dent had hit one in a playoff game against the Red Sox on October 2, 1978. Kirk Gibson had his in the '88 World Series, when Jack Buck couldn't believe what he just saw. And in the regular season, there had been the night when Henry Aaron had hit No. 715 in old Atlanta Fulton County Stadium, taking the all-time home-run record from Ruth, Aaron on his way to 755 before he retired.

Not one of them was known as the shot heard 'round the world.

"It wasn't just me," Thomson said. "Who was I? It was everything. It was New York, it was the Giants versus the Dodgers, it was the way we'd come from so far behind [13 ½ games in August that year], it was the fact that we came from behind that day [4–2 behind] in the bottom of the ninth. It was eight teams in the National League instead of all the ones they have now. It was the World Series on the line. You tell me my home run is safe today and maybe you're right. Sometimes it's like that ball I hit never came down."

Thomson said, "I was just talking about this with a friend the other day. I still get quite a bit of mail. Answer it all, too."

He said he would watch as much of these games the next few nights, more baseball than he was used to watching, because now he was caught up in the whole thing the way everybody else was. He talked again about how different it was in '51, how he wasn't expected to do what he did, how it was do-or-die, he either kept the game going or he didn't; but how he did remember, in the back of his head, that he had hit a home run off Branca in Game 1 of that Giants–Dodger series, one that Branca had started. Then he told me something he had told me before, pride creeping into his voice now, about how a lot of people have had the chance to deliver in moments like these, all across baseball history, especially in October.

But he had delivered.

He had that swing in him.

"Hey," Thomson said, "I don't take credit for a lot of things that have happened to me. But I had the ability to make that swing. I gave myself a chance to do something great."

He did. Let the other guys have their chance now. Like Roger Maris's friend had said: Somebody else's turn. Thirty-seven years after Maris, forty-seven years after the Polo Grounds, Bobby Thomson said, "How could a little guy like me be treated like a big shot this long?"

Thomson said he would watch and see if McGwire ran around the bases as fast as he had run in '51, if he would come flying the last ninety feet between third and home and then disappear into his whole team, waiting there for him at the plate, like a halfback disappearing into the line at the goal line in football. He would be interested to see who ended up with the ball; all this time later, no one knew what had happened to the ball Thomson hit off Branca in the Polo Grounds.

And he said that in all probability, he would watch McGwire go for No. 62 at home.

"If he does it this week," Bobby Thomson said, "it'll be easy for me to remember where I was when he did."

"You have to let us stay up," Christopher said.

"You *have* to," Alex said.

Alex backs his older brother up on anything, by reflex, voting the straight Chris ticket, on all matters. Especially one like this, with McGwire sitting on 61 home runs and the Cardinals–Cubs game coming on at eight o'clock Eastern time. The lobbying—it was a school night—had begun when they had gotten out of bed in the morning. Actually, it had begun the night before, Labor Day, after McGwire had hit 61 against Mike Morgan of the Cubs.

"You can watch the start of the game and then we'll see," I said. "Maybe he'll hit it first time up, and then you guys won't have a problem."

"What if he doesn't?" Alex said.

He had been carrying his McGwire card around all weekend, taking it with us to Shea Stadium on Saturday afternoon when we had gone to see the Mets play. We had killed time across the street, watching some of the U.S. Open tennis at Arthur Ashe Stadium, but it was only an overture to Saturday afternoon. This was a baseball day, with tickets behind the Mets dugout. The Mets were still fighting for a playoff spot in the National League, and so every game was a big game for them by the first weekend of September. And the boys knew that whatever happened with McGwire in St. Louis—he had been stuck on 59 for a couple of days, which by now felt like an eternity—they would surely be able to follow it on the television screen in the outfield.

"You're sure we won't miss it?" Zach said.

I told him I was pretty sure they would want to show the people if McGwire got to 60 today.

"I want to really see this one, Dad," Chris said.

Meaning he didn't want me to have to pull over on the parkway on the way home.

"You'll see it," I assured them all.

But in a way, they heard it first at Shea Stadium. This time from all the radios people had brought to the place, listening to the all-news stations, knowing that they would break in with the news of No. 60. The news of 60 on this day moved through the stands at Shea like some lit fuse, before we saw anything on the scoreboard, before any announcement was made over the public address system. The people with transistor radios—like the one permanently under my pillow, attached to my ear in September and into October of '61—knew about McGwire and so did the ones who had brought one of those small battery-powered television sets, the kind Chris wanted to bring with him so he could watch the Cardinals–Reds game on Fox.

Sixty, you heard at Shea in the very first inning of the Mets–Braves game.

He hit *sixty.*

Not the name, McGwire.

Just the number, still magic.

So we really did hear the home run before we saw it, as if the cheers had made their way from one ballpark to another, from St. Louis all the way to New York. If we could not be in the ballpark with McGwire, at least we were in a ballpark, and it seemed important. Now they were making the announcement over the p.a. system, and it was all official that McGwire had gotten to 60 faster than Ruth had in 1927, faster than Maris had in '61. Across the country, my boys and I stood up along with everybody else in the ballpark and gave a standing ovation to Mark McGwire, one that seemed to go on and on.

This was the sound of baseball, loud and clear, as clear as the day, on our own baseball Saturday. It was not as loud as Busch Stadium, but loud enough.

We cheered No. 60, which had been the magic number for thirty-four years until Maris changed things, by one, on October 1, 1961, two years exactly before McGwire was born. We cheered the number because Ruth had made it so big for so long. In 1927, on the day he hit No. 60 off Tom Zachary of the Washington Senators, Ruth had cheered himself, loud and clear.

"Sixty!" he yelled in the Yankee clubhouse that day. "Count 'em. Sixty! Let's see some other SOB match that."

It took Maris such a long time. It took even longer between Maris and McGwire. But now it had happened again. McGwire had gotten there in the Cardinals' 143rd game, at the beginning of September instead of the end. In St. Louis, Jack Buck shouted, "Move over, Babe!" on the radio. That was September 5, and then on September 7 came No. 61, and it was Maris who had to move over.

Now it was September 8, and it was the same on this night as it had been at Roger Dean Stadium in the spring.

Alex said, "Do you really think he's going to hit one today?"

Before I could answer Alex said, "I definitely think he's going to."

There was no urgency. Still three weeks of season to go. Plenty of time. But the networks were covering McGwire and Sosa as if these were the last days of a presidential campaign, and now everybody had gotten lucky because the two of them were in the same park. It had been completely different in '61, all of it, because as big as Ruth's record was, sports wasn't as big then, the media wasn't as big, there wasn't as much television, a million channels in the night, and all-sports radio, all the time, blowing one hole after another in the ozone. There was no coverage like this, never this kind of hype surrounding Maris and Mantle, this kind of buildup. My friends and I followed it, every day, of course. I think back now, and it is as if the whole summer was spent either listening to the Yankees, watching them on the weekends, playing ball on the field that was right next to our house, at the end of Earl Avenue in Oneida, New York, one that looks impossibly small now when I take my sons to see it, a postage stamp of green even though I remember it as being as wide and spacious as Yankee Stadium. It was all baseball that year. A Harvey Kuenn glove with a hole in the pocket, finally, from too much oil. A regulation bat my father had bought for me the Christmas before, the only thing I saw under the tree that morning, a bat I remember now as being almost white as the snow outside. A Yankee cap. Home runs and baseball games and all that, as if it was all one piece.

But there was urgency at the end. When Maris sat on 60, there was just one game left, against the Red Sox at the Stadium. It was that day or never.

Then there was the ball in the air, on the black-and-white television at my aunt's house, and the sound of Phil Rizzuto's voice calling Maris's shot, and that was the end of it.

"Someday you'll tell your own kids about this," my father said, because he said that to me a lot, on the first day of October and the last real day of summer in 1961, when I was nine.

So now I watched with a boy who would turn eleven in a week and an eight-year-old and Zach, who made it through the first three innings. Then it was just Chris and Alex and me, alone with baseball.

Alex did what he always did for the big games. He surrounded himself with his stuff. He had a box of autographed balls. He had two thick binders of baseball cards. He had the McGwire card out, separate. If he was right, if McGwire did it tonight, then he was completely prepared. But by then we all were. The day before, I had talked to NBC's Bob Costas. We were the same age, and had been in each other's weddings. He lived in St. Louis now, and went to Cardinals games all the time, and would be working the American League Championship Series for NBC. But until then, he had no games to do, and so he sat in the stands at Busch Stadium and watched this great story unfold in front of his eyes, sometimes sitting in the first row of the stands, and wasn't able to make a single call, wasn't able to say anything.

He had also come out of the summer of '61. But he had grown up in Commack, and so he had gotten to root for Mickey Mantle in person that summer, gotten to see some of those home runs with his own eyes. And then walked across the field with the rest of the fans when the game was over.

"I know what I'd say if I got to call No. 62," Costas said.

And then over the telephone, one of the most famous sports

voices in the country gave an imaginary call of a home run not yet hit, playing to an audience of one.

"... and that ball is history" is the way Costa's call ended.

We waited for the history in front of the television set. My boys and I. It was a school night and I had promised them at least two at bats for McGwire, and then I said we'd see after that.

"You got to see Maris," Chris said.

"I told you, it was a Sunday afternoon."

"So?"

"What if he hits it right after we go to bed, how would you feel then?" Alex said. Dealing the guilt card. Somehow they're born knowing how.

I smiled at both of them. "I'd feel as if I'd missed it, same as you did."

We didn't miss it.

The cameras nearly did in the bottom of the fourth, with Steve Trachsel pitching for the Cubs, just because the ball was hit so low, and disappeared over the wall so quickly. But Alex knew first. He sees a bite in boxing and everything with those amazing eyes, and he jumped up, binders and cards and baseballs flying, and yelled, "He did it!"

"Oh yeah!" Chris yelled. "Number sixty-two, baby!"

I hugged one and then the other. Then I had them both with me on the couch as we watched McGwire with his own son, Matt, at home plate. And I told my sons that someday they would tell their sons about this night.

Then Chris said, "Let's call Poppa."

Their name for my father.

"You think he's still up?" Alex said.

I told them there was a pretty good chance he was.

Chris made the call, and I heard him say, "Did you see, Poppa?"

It wasn't long before my Chris had his hand over the phone.

"Poppa started to talk about McGwire holding up his son at the plate and then I think maybe he started to cry," he said.

Then he was talking fast and loud to his grandfather and laughing and they were both reviewing the same pictures they were seeing on television, and then Alex was on the phone doing the same thing, about the newest set of images. The replays of Cardinals first base coach Dave McKay frantically yelling for McGwire to come back and touch first base.

McGwire in the stands with Roger Maris's children.

Sosa running in from the outfield and McGwire lifting him as easily as Mark McGwire had lifted his son.

Finally I got the phone.

In the background, on his television, I heard the voices of Joe Buck and Tim McCarver, crazy with this moment the way Phil Rizzuto had been in '61.

"I wish you could have been here with us, Pop," I said.

"I was," my father said. "I was."

I reminded him that he had always told me that someday somebody else would come along and beat Maris.

"Your father," he said, "is always right. Isn't that what I always taught you?"

"Hey, Pop," I said, and then I was going to tell him all about it, about boyhood and summers and baseball and still being his kid, never more so than on a night like this. Just because it was that kind of night, and we were connected to it and to each other by more than the telephone by the same old golden thread.

Then I was the one who couldn't get the words out, the way he couldn't with Christopher, his first grandson.

"We just wanted to call" was the best I could do.

"Did Zach go to bed?" my dad said.

"A while ago."

"Don't forget to write him a note," my father said, and hung up.

I wrote that note, much later, when the game was finally over, and the interviews had all been given, and the replays had already begun on ESPN and all the rest of the channels, and the whole world must have felt it had seen McGwire go tearing around first base without touching it a hundred times, and Matt McGwire seemed to have spent more time in the air at Busch Stadium than all of his father's home runs combined.

I wrote Zach his note, and it said what his brothers had said:

Dear Zach-o:
He did it!
No. 62, baby!
Your dad.

No need for notes with the others. Someday they would tell their own children. They would remember the night exactly. I stopped in both bedrooms before going to bed myself, watched them sleep the way I had watched them sleep a hundred other nights, or maybe a thousand, looked around at the caps and gloves and pictures and pennants and balls and general marvelous mess of childhood and dreams. Chris had propped his Tino Martinez bat, the one Tino had signed for his tenth birthday, against the end of the bed where he slept.

Alex had the McGwire card in his hand.

MATT WILLIAMS WOULD NOT REMEMBER MCGWIRE'S ball in the air, diving over the left-field wall the way it did. He would remember the son in the air.

He looked at the father and the son at home plate, and only then did Williams see himself there, just for a moment. Only then did Williams, who chased Roger Maris himself once, allow himself to wonder what might have been in the Summer of '94, not '98, if the baseball strike had not ended the season and his own chance to be a baseball immortal.

But on the night of McGwire's 62nd, Williams watched on television the way the country watched and remembered the boy, Matt McGwire, up there against the sky in his father's arms.

McGwire is a divorced parent, and so is Matt Williams. Williams has two daughters and a son, Jacob, seven years old. He loves them all, saw all of them in the air.

Fathers and sons. And daughters.

"You ask me what was special about Mark's night," Williams says, "and I will tell you it was seeing a father at home plate with his kid."

Once, in '94, when Williams was playing third base for the San Francisco Giants, hitting in the same batting order with Barry Bonds, he had 43 home runs in August, August 12, to be exact. There were still 50 games left for him to play. With 50 games to play in the '98 season, McGwire had 45 home runs. It meant he was two home runs ahead of Williams's pace.

Two home runs.

So that summer we were doing the math on Matt Williams, tracking where he stood with Ruth and Maris, measuring his pace against that of Ken Griffey, Jr., who had 40 in August, and even Bonds, who had gotten very hot and moved up to 37. We were wondering if Williams could get to 50 by September 1—why not? seven home runs in three weeks? why in the world not?—and if he did, how he would stand up to the force of the media and history and the spotlight of the country as he got closer to Maris.

Then the players walked out on August 12th, striking against the owners, and while no one knew it for sure that night, it was the end of baseball in 1994. No more home runs for Williams or anybody. No World Series.

No baseball until the spring.

Wait till next year.

Only, that was Williams's year. He never came close to having another one like it. That was the magic time for him. That was his shot at a perfect summer.

"It just seemed that wherever we went," Williams says now, at the end of someone else's home-run season, "the wind was always blowing out."

Then the players went out, and that is why four years later, Williams doesn't expect much sympathy. "I was one of the guys who voted to strike," he says. "So I can never say anybody took anything away from me."

He is one of the stand-up guys of his sport, always has been; a gentleman of baseball. He would say that. But in his heart, Williams knows something: There would have been a strike if he had voted to keep playing. There was nothing he could do. It was all out of his hands. No matter what, the bat was out of his hands. And so he would always wonder how those 50 games would have gone, how soon he would have gotten to 50 home runs, what September would have been like if he had stayed healthy and hot. Would he have turned for home with the great closing burst we got from both McGwire and Sosa?

Would he have been able to smile?

Would there finally have been a night when he touched home plate with all his children in his arms and touched us all the way Mark and Matt McGwire did?

It is so easy to forget '94 now, because of the strike. But that was another special season in baseball. Williams had 33 home runs at the All-Star break; so did Griffey; and Frank Thomas of the White Sox had 32. Then Bonds joined the party with six home runs in ten games before everything came to a stop.

"I guess I was on a pace for sixty-two or sixty-three," Williams says. "The way I was going, was hitting nineteen home runs in fifty games possible? Sure it was. But it just wasn't the same for me, or Kenny or Barry. Because no matter how many home runs I hit, there was always the cloud of the strike hanging over the season. There was a part of me never believing I'd get the chance to go the distance."

He was traded to the Indians from the Giants, and got to play in a World Series. Then he was traded to the expansion Arizona Diamondbacks. In the years between his home-run summer and McGwire's, he was divorced from his wife Tracie. Forced to live apart from Alysha, Rachael, Jacob.

"When you're a professional athlete and you're married, you take so much for granted," he says. "You go on the road, but you know that when you come back, your family will be there waiting for you. You take for granted that your wife will be there and, every single time you come back, everything will be fine. Then one day everything isn't fine, and your kids aren't always there for you."

He says, "That's why watching McGwire with his son was so meaningful to me."

He wanted the Diamondbacks, because it meant he could be closer to his children, living in Arizona with their mother. He wanted the Diamondbacks, even though he knew he would be going from the World Series to last place, to a team starting at the bottom, the way all expansion teams do. Which the Diamondbacks did, starting out 8–31 in their first season. On the night McGwire hit No. 62, Matt Williams, Diamondbacks third baseman, had 18 home runs. Williams watched McGwire reach these heights from the bottom of the National League West.

He watched and saw things from Busch Stadium that the rest of us didn't see.

That fathers like me, lucky enough to watch with their sons, did not see.

And perhaps this was part of the beauty of the summer, too, part of baseball's deep and amazing pull on us all, no matter where we were watching. Williams had gone two-thirds of the way up McGwire's mountain once; he had at least seen some of the view from there. He knew what the air was like up there. But now, in another summer, with another team, on the other side of the mountain in his baseball life, Williams had a different view, a different perspective.

Of course, a part of him wanted to hit No. 62. Make that swing. Only, he found out something on the night of No. 62. He had let go of 1994. He was a father on this night, not an ex–home run king. He wanted to be where I was, watching with his kids.

It is funny how these things work out sometimes.

Matt Williams could not take his eyes off Matt McGwire.

BACK HOME IN THE DOMINICAN REPUBLIC, THEY never took their eyes off Sammy Sosa. And they did not take their eyes off Sosa in New York City's Washington Heights, which has the largest Dominican population this side of Santo Domingo. If Fargo, North Dakota, was still Maris country, Washington Heights was Sosa country. He was still the home-run hero, even if McGwire had broken the record first. If Sammy Sosa could hit all those home runs in June, if he could hit a home run almost every day for a month, then they knew his bat still had home runs in it in September.

No ballplayer alive could have gone toe-to-toe with McGwire in St. Louis during that Cardinals–Cubs series. This was McGwire's park, McGwire's turf, McGwire's crowd. McGwire's moment. At least for that moment. More than ever, Sosa made himself into the best supporting actor in this extraordinary miniseries. Mostly he did this by trying to hit everything the Cardinals threw him all the way into the Mississippi River. He brought grace to the occasion, as he had since June. Just not with a bat in his hands. He smiled, he said the right things, he acted like a happy kid who had hopped the fence when he came running for McGwire after the historic home run.

Sosa just did not hit. For a couple of days, it was finally like some sort of heavyweight fight, and McGwire had hit him. Knocked him down and maybe out.

Not everyone thought that way.

"We were all excited for McGwire," a man named Gabe Rosario says in Washington Heights on September 13, five days after McGwire had hit No. 62. "But in our hearts we believed Sammy could still catch him."

Rosario is forty-nine years old. He is the floor manager at a place called Coogan's, at 169th and Broadway in Washington Heights, in the heart of this place that is like a Little Santo Domingo. Rosario was born in San Francisco de Macoris in the Dominican Republic. He grew up with all the romantic ideas about baseball, about making it in baseball, about baseball taking him to America and the big leagues the way it had Sosa, coming out of San Pedro de Macoris; about making it to Yankee Stadium and playing center field for the New York Yankees the way Mickey Mantle and the great Joe DiMaggio had. And he became a good, solid ballplayer back home, playing for professional teams like Hogar Macorisano (the Macoris Hometowners) and Ayuntamiento Municipal (the City Hall Team).

But he was one who never made it out. Never made it big the way so many others from his country had made it. Never had the flash that some of the others had, or the talent. So his name did not go up in lights with the Alous, with Juan Marichal and Manny Mota, Pedro Guerrero and Cesar Cedeno, George Bell and Alfredo Griffin and Tony Fernandez and Joaquin Andujar, this amazing list of people from his country who would enrich major-league baseball in the last forty years of the century, make all baseball boys in the Dominican pick up a bat and glove and dream.

He would never catch the eye of a scout like Amado Dinzey, one who would make the call that Dinzey made to Omar Minaya.

"For all the ones who make it," Gabe Rosario says, "there are all the ones like me."

By the time he made it to New York City, he was twenty-seven years old, and the only baseball he played was in softball leagues in Central Park. He followed the game, but not the way he used to, certainly not the way he had when he was growing up. He made a life for himself in New York, a good life; he became part of the marvelous diverse New York family that was Coogan's, the Irish bar with Rosario working the floor and Suzie Rodriguez the bar; Suzie was out of Santiago, the second city of the Dominican Republic, and was about to begin a full-time teaching job in the New York City public school system in September of '98. It was an Irish bar surrounded by bodegas, with baseball spoken on the television set on summer nights and Spanish spoken outside on the streets.

Baseball was still important to Gabe Rosario, just not as important as it had been. So he was a little bit like his adopted country that way. Baseball was still important, just not as important as it had been before the strike in August of '94.

But now Gabe Rosario had this baseball summer.

More important, he had Sosa.

Sosa: having this season out of Gabe Rosario's imagination.

"From the time he got hot and got close to McGwire," Rosario says, "he has been in my heart."

Never more than on Sunday afternoon, the thirteenth of September, when Sosa let everyone know that he was still in the game.

SOSA HAD GOTTEN BACK TO WRIGLEY, GOTTEN HOT.

On Friday, the eleventh, he had hit No. 59, off Bill Pulsipher of the Milwaukee Brewers.

On Saturday, it was No. 60, putting him in the club with Ruth and Maris and McGwire, off Valerio De Los Santos of the Brewers.

McGwire was still at 62, seemingly drained by all the excitement and emotion of getting there earlier in the week. Suddenly, he was the one who seemed to have been hit by the whole long chase, and seemed to be swinging a hockey stick at the ball, at least temporarily. So once again there was an opening for Sosa.

Now, on this Sunday afternoon, Sosa, still playing against the Brewers, had hit No. 61, off Bronswell Patrick. He was even with Maris now. He was one away from McGwire. The Maris family wasn't in the ballpark, the balls hadn't been specially marked—or, more specifically, Marked—and the country wasn't focused on this game, certainly not on a pro football Sunday in America.

They were focused enough in Washington Heights, New York City, on a sun-splashed day that felt more like the beginning of the summer in New York than the end. As soon as the word spread out of windows and up and down the streets that Sosa had hit one, the car horns began to blare and everywhere you could see "Sosa 61" written in the back windows of cars, and suddenly you saw more and more people on the streets, smiling, full of the news about Sosa.

The Cubs–Brewers game was not being shown on national television. One of the sets at Coogan's was showing golf. Then ESPN was cutting into the game at Wrigley because Sosa had hit No. 62, off a veteran right-hander named Eric Plunk, who had once been McGwire's teammate with the Oakland A's.

"Some people cheered," Suzie Rodriguez would say. "Some people cried."

There was more noise from the street, the streets around upper Broadway sounding now like another part of the city, Times Square on New Year's Eve. As if Sosa's ball landing beyond the ivy at

Wrigley was like the ball falling in Times Square. As if Rosa were ringing in one last round to his fight with McGwire.

One last time, two weeks to go in the season, they were even. McGwire 62, Sosa 62.

Dave Hunt, who owns Coogan's, had walked out of the place a few minutes before Sosa went deep against Plunk. Hunt had been busy all day, remembered he hadn't even bought the Sunday papers yet. As he came out of a bodega, papers under his arm, he thought he saw a mistake on the back window of a livery cab.

It said "Sosa 62."

Hunt would say, "I start doing the math in my head, because when I left the bar I was sure Sosa was still one behind. Now I'm wondering if McGwire had hit No. 63 the other night in St. Louis when we all went crazy. But then I heard what was going on inside the joint, and I realized that Sammy'd caught him."

"We really do think of this as Little Santo Domingo," Hunt said later that night. "All of a sudden, out of nowhere, it was a baseball holiday."

Gabe Rosario hugged Suzie Rodriguez on the day when Sosa hit No. 62 and tied Mark McGwire. Gabe Rosario was one of those crying at Coogan's, and he would cry later when he sat at the end of the bar and watched another replay. He had not given up on Sosa, because no one in this neighborhood had, no one back home in Santo Domingo and San Pedro de Macoris and San Francisco de Macoris and Santiago, Suzie's hometown, had given up. They had seen too much by now; Sosa had carried them all this far.

"They must be dancing in the streets," Gabe Rosario said. "Maybe I will do a little dance myself tonight."

He said, "I won't have to go to the dancing clubs, either. I think all I will have to do is walk outside."

Sosa's 62nd, coming five days after McGwire's, coming when

we all seemed stuck in some sort of home-run hangover the way McGwire himself was, did not bring the country to a sudden stop the way McGwire's 62nd had. Again: So much of this was Sosa's doing. He had positioned himself as the Other Guy. He had made that role a perfect fit, smiling through it all, touching his heart, blowing his kisses on days when he hit home runs and when he did not.

No one was calling Sosa a national hero, which is what McGwire had been called all week, on television, in the sports pages, on the radio, on the editorial pages of all important newspapers. But the more Sosa shared the stage with McGwire, the more people saw him smile and make McGwire smile along with him—the more people saw Sosa bring an old-fashioned quality known as grace to this re-markable production—he began to emerge as a hero himself, in the Dominican Republic and in America as well, a new kind of national hero in a changing America. If that all sounds lofty, it is because it fit the day, fit the season, a season still played in mid-September in such a lofty place.

"I cheer today for my brother," Gabe Rosario said on September 13, 1998.

He went outside the bar to drink in more of the day. There seemed to be music and noise everywhere, outside Coogan's and outside the bodegas on Audubon Avenue. In the early evening, when everyone knew what Sosa had done, the traffic was thick on upper Broadway and on Fort George Hill, where the people used to look out the windows and see another great young Dominican ballplayer, Manny Ramirez of the Cleveland Indians, training by running the hill with a tire around his waist. To make him strong, the way Sosa was strong. It takes strength to carry a country, or two. It really was a baseball holiday now in Washington Heights, far from Wrigley Field and far from the real Santo Domingo. Washington Heights is the highest geographical point in the city of New York. On this Sunday, it felt like the highest point in baseball, the air as clean and intoxicating as the top of a mountain, at the top of the world.

THAT NIGHT, WE SAT AND WATCHED THE HIGH-lights of Sosa's day at Wrigley. Zach asked a question that Alex had asked in the spring.

"If they end up tied, who has the record?"

"They both have the record."

"McGwire got there first."

"He did," I said. "So technically, McGwire broke Roger Maris's record and then Sammy tied McGwire."

Alex had gone to bed early, which was always a surprise with him, because he is always looking for five extra minutes, whether there is a game on or not. But he had disappeared, looking serious. Somehow he had become a Sosa man as the summer wore on. When he would get a big hit in the backyard, even clear the swimming-pool fence in the home-run derby games, he would touch his heart, blow his kiss. He had Sosa down cold.

When he was asleep, I went quietly into his room to see what he had been doing, what secret work he had found for himself up there. Everything is deep and secret and important with Alex.

I found one of those old black-and-white Mead Square Deal composition books, the kind you first use in grammar school, with the "Class Schedule" on the inside front cover. Somehow, across my life, I had kept using them as notebooks, even in my job as a columnist. On my desk, in drawers, in shelves, there were stacks and stacks of them, going back across the years, filled with notes and interviews and the starts of columns and parts of columns and phone numbers.

Alex used them, too, in school, as diaries. He had them scattered all over his own room. Most of them had "Alex's Journal" on the front in big letters.

Some of them had "Do Not Open!" on them.

Next to his bed was a new one.

I opened it up.

At the top of the page, he had written "Sammy Sosa 21," as if that were Sosa's autograph. It was as if he had tried to copy it off a baseball card, or out of one of the *Beckett's* magazines he and his brother kept, ones telling them how much their cards were worth.

And then underneath Sosa's name, again and again, he had written his own name, with his number, 11, from the Ontarios. The way he had written it across the card from him I carried in my wallet.

In the morning, I showed him the page, asked him what he had been doing.

He smiled right off the card.

"Practicing my autograph," he said.

A season written in the heart, wherever you watched the home runs, wherever you were born, however young or old you were.

· *seven* ·

September

(second half)

THE DAY BEFORE, WE HAD BEEN AT SHEA STADIUM.
I had asked Christopher what he wanted to do most for his
birthday—he had turned eleven on Thursday—and he said he
wanted to go to a ball game. He is Yankees all the way, has been since
he first cared about baseball, but he said the Mets–Marlins game
would be fine. The Mets were fighting with Sosa's Cubs and the Giants for the wild-card playoff spot in the National League, and so
every game was like a playoff game for them now.

"I want to see at least one more game in person," he said.

I told him it was done, that the deal was the same as it had been
all season, when I saw how baseball had taken over the house, the

whole summer, the whole country: if somebody wanted to go to a game on the weekends and I could swing it, we would go.

Chris brought along a friend from school. We sat in the same seats, close to the field, where Alex had sat for his birthday. In the fifth inning, the Mets put "Happy Birthday, Christopher Lupica" up on the scoreboard. I didn't tell him it was coming. His friend, Conner O'Rourke—up where we live in Connecticut, we lead the league in Conors—saw it first and pounded him on the shoulder, and then they were both looking out there now as if somebody had hit some monster home run that was bouncing off Chris's name.

When his name was gone, replaced by the next birthday greeting, he looked over at me.

"Who did that?" he said.

"The baseball gods."

In a few days, the Mets would collapse completely, lose their last five games, miss being in a tie with the Cubs and Giants for the wild card by one game. But they were still alive on this day. So was the ballpark. The night before, the Mets' closer, John Franco, had blown a lead in the ninth inning, blown the game, been responsible for a loss that had run over his team like a bus.

And now, three hours into this game, with the Mets holding a 4–3 lead, Mets manager Bobby Valentine brought Franco in to pitch the ninth again.

Some people at Shea booed. A lot of people booed. Valentine was out talking to the home-plate umpire when Franco began jogging in from the bullpen, and now the Mets' manager turned his back to the umpire and home plate and gestured for the people in the house to get up and cheer Franco. Waved his arms like a cheerleader. Valentine knew he had to get his closer—37 saves for Franco to that point—back in there right away, give him the ball fast after what had happened the night before. But he also knew that he might be putting his team's season on the line.

Far from McGwire's home-run season, far from Sosa's, was this bright, loud moment. No one here knew that the Mets were doomed. All we had in the ballpark was this inning, this game; everything was riding on whatever Franco would do next.

Chris Lupica sat on the back of his chair, cap turned around on his head, as excited about this as anything he had seen in baseball all season. McGwire or Sosa or anything. Because this was it, this was the best of it right in front of him, every pitch feeling as if it meant the world.

"How great is this?" he yelled over the crowd at Conner O'Rourke.

The inning seemed to take an hour. By the end, we were all on our feet at Shea. Franco was all over the place with his pitches. Todd Dunwoody led off the ninth for the Marlins. Franco walked him. More booing. Then Mark Kotsay hit a ball that deflected off Franco's glove to Rey Ordonez, the spectacular Mets shortstop. Somehow Ordonez charged the ball and reached for it and threw it in the same sleight-of-hand motion and got Kotsay at first, Dunwoody taking second on the play.

Maybe Franco would get out of this, after all.

Then he walked Derrek Lee.

He got Cliff Floyd to pop up to third. With two outs, he hit Kevin Orie with a pitch.

Mets still leading, 4–3.

Bases loaded.

Mike Redmond, a backup catcher for the Marlins, at the plate.

Somehow, the count went to 3–2 on Redmond.

A season that had begun for me back in Jupiter with all my sons, all of us screaming our heads off for McGwire to hit one out, had come down to this at Shea Stadium, Chris and Conner and I screaming our heads off for Franco to throw a strike past Redmond.

It was one of those baseball moments, one out of all the ones in your life, that seem ridiculously exciting.

Franco, who grew up in Brooklyn and used to sneak into Shea with his brother Jimmy when they both were Chris and Conner's age, threw a change-up in the dirt. It would have been ball four. Redmond swung at it and missed. The place exploded. Perfect ending, at least.

At the beginning of the inning, I had asked a couple of security guys I know at Shea if we could jump over the wall, run out the tunnel behind home plate, and make a fast getaway to where the car was parked. They said sure. As everybody else kept cheering Franco, the security guys helped us over the fence and then we were on the field.

We ran for the tunnel, but just before we got there, Chris stopped.

Turning to take one more look, one more snapshot for the corner of imagination where the special sports memories are stored. The Mets still mobbing Franco on the field. All the ones in the stands who didn't want to leave yet, to let go of this one game or the top of the ninth.

The scoreboard where his name had been.

The whole day and night on his face.

Taking in the sights and sounds and feel of it all, looking down at the grass behind home plate, the way his grandfather had looked down at the outfield grass that time at Yankee Stadium. This was the first time Christopher had ever stood on a major-league field. So he had made it a lot sooner than Bene Lupica had.

"Come on, pal," I said finally. "We gotta move."

He took a big deep breath.

"This is the best birthday of my whole life," he said, and then we ran for the car.

On the ride home, he and Conner replayed every pitch of the ninth inning as we listened to the Mets' postgame show on the radio.

For this one night, we did not talk about home runs, or about the Yankees, even though Chris would usually rather talk about the Yankees than even about the girl who played Buffy the Vampire Slayer. We talked about the Mets and Franco and what it had been like to have a ninth inning like that close enough to touch.

"Screw up one day, be a hero the next," Conner O'Rourke said.

"Don't you feel like somebody new does something great every single day?" Chris Lupica, now eleven, said from the backseat.

The next night, Cal Ripken, Jr., did something.

He finally sat down.

WE WERE ACTUALLY GETTING READY TO WATCH pro football on this night after the long weekend of baseball. *Sunday Night Football* on ESPN. Chris especially loved to watch the highlight show that came before, *NFL Prime Time*, following the best plays and games of the day while the host, Chris Berman, told you all about it in his carnival barker's voice.

But before we sat down for that, my office called. Peter Botte, who covers the Yankees for the *Daily News,* had called to tell the guys on the desk that Cal Ripken, Jr., had walked into the office of Orioles manager Ray Miller and told him he was taking a night off, sitting out a game for the first time in sixteen years.

After Ripken had played 2,632 straight games for the Orioles.

"It's time," Ripken had said to Miller.

Just like that.

Miller had crossed out Ripken's name from the starting lineup and replaced it with Ryan Minor's.

My editor wanted to know if I wanted to write.

I told him I had already started.

Thinking back to a February afternoon a few years earlier, before Ripken had broken Lou Gehrig's streak for consecutive games.

I was writing a magazine article on Ripken, and he had invited me to his home outside Baltimore, and now he was showing me around the property.

"You want to see the gym, right?" he said, grinning.

I told him that was all I really wanted to see.

I had read about the converted barn on Ripken's property. Seen pictures of it. Now I was standing inside it. Like the first ticketholder of the day entering his personal magic kingdom: Ripken World. The basketball court, a full basketball court, with the real electronic scoreboard up in the balcony. Behind the scoreboard was a room full of weights and exercise equipment. On the same level as the basketball court, in a smaller area, was Ripken's batting cage, an antique Iron Mike that his father, Cal Ripken, Sr., had restored for him to perfect, spit-polished working order.

"Having a place like this has always been a dream of mine," he said that day.

I told him, "I was thinking of taking my kids to Disney World next month. But if you don't mind, I think we'll just come here."

He laughed and asked if I'd brought my sneakers, as he'd told me to over the phone. I told him they were in my rental car. "Go get 'em," he said. "We'll shoot around before lunch. It'll help me start getting loose for the game later."

During the off-season, Ripken had a game almost every single day on this court. He had still not caught Gehrig. He had managed to make it through a dozen seasons without getting hurt in baseball. One of the ways he stayed fit in the winter was with basketball. It was in his contract that he could play these games. So he did. Six days a week, every week he was in town. He had a Monday-Wednesday-Friday group. He had Tuesday-Thursday-Saturday players. Old friends. Local high school kids if they were good enough. College kids.

But always serious ball.

No one more serious than the host.

He said he always invited ten other players besides himself, making eleven in all.

"So you have a substitute in case somebody gets hurt?" I said.

Ripken grinned.

"Actually," he said, "it's so we always have one guy running the scoreboard."

I went and got my sneakers and we shot around for a while. Ripken in basketball was a revelation, even goofing around while he warmed up. He is so serious on a ballfield, almost solemn. On this basketball court, his private, lavish dream playground, he was all boy. Going behind his back. Laughing and dribbling between his legs. Rolling the ball down his arm and onto his fingertip like a Globetrotter. And dunking. Dunking big-time.

"You want to play some one-on-one?" he asked.

Now I laughed.

"Not really."

"Come on," Cal Ripken said. "For fun."

It was fun for exactly one shot. He backed off and gave me an open three. Which I nearly made.

The next time I got the ball, he came out to check it the way you do in playground ball. And stayed right there, in my eyeballs. In perfect defensive position. As if waiting for the pitcher to pitch at Camden Yards.

I said something like, What's this?

"Defense," he said.

It was a game, that was all he knew. He played hard every basket and killed me, and played hard later on when the real players showed up. It was all he knew and all he had ever known across all the seasons when he played every day, when he got ready for the seasons playing on his own court, working out in his own gym, hitting against his own hitting machine.

"I never set out to make history," he said that day.

We did not talk much about Gehrig's record. He knew he would break it and I knew he would break it, and it was just a matter of how the schedule would fall in 1995, what night it would be, what game, what opponent. All he did say at lunch was this:

"Someday when it's all over you can write this. Someday it will be time. No one will have to tell me. I'll tell them."

Now he had told everybody, three years after the September when everything was about him. It wasn't home-run hitters who made people celebrate baseball that year. It was Ripken doing that, one year after the strike of '94 had killed a season and a World Series and, some said, killed baseball as the national pastime forever. There was finally the night of September 6 and Ripken played in his 2,131st consecutive game and Gehrig's record, the one that would never be broken, had been broken.

The country stopped for Ripken that night, the way it would stop the night of McGwire's 62nd. It was one of those nights in sports that seem to go on forever, and nobody seemed to mind, because baseball had waited longer for someone to pass Gehrig than it had waited for someone to pass Roger Maris.

Ripken's time. The ceremonies were about him. He was the one who touched off a national celebration of baseball, thirteen months after he and the rest of the players were supposed to have ruined baseball with their strike. There were fireworks for him at Camden Yards, speeches on the field and presentations and tears. Now, sixteen years after the streak had begun, it had all ended without any fireworks, ended as quietly as it had begun in 1982, ended with the understated dignity that Ripken had brought to every day and night of his baseball life.

He told them it was time and sat in the dugout with the rest of the Orioles' substitutes. He did what he told me once was the hardest thing for him to do in this world: watch the game instead of play it.

We were in Fort Lauderdale the day he said it, the spring after he broke Gehrig's record. The Orioles had themselves a pretty good team, and would make it all the way to the American League Championship Series before losing to the Yankees. Davey Johnson was the Orioles' manager. It was clear that the Orioles were going to be a contender; that Ripken might have his best shot at going back to the World Series for the first time since 1983. And in the Orioles' clubhouse that day, one that had belonged to the Yankees before they moved their spring training home across the state to Tampa, Ripken talked about throwing out the first pitch of the World Series the previous October, in Atlanta.

"I felt funny throwing out that first pitch," Ripken said. "It was such an honor, but I'm still playing and it's always something I've associated with people who've retired. And it's not as if I'd forgotten what the World Series is like."

He paused, leaned against an exercise machine. He probably had the same one in the gym above the basketball court back home.

"But since '83," he said, "I'd just watched the Series on television. Now here it was all around me. I can feel the excitement the players are feeling. I can feel the pressure."

Ripken said, "I spent the whole night wishing I was out there playing."

Now he had taken himself out, to remove the pressure from himself and his team once and for all, to do it in front of a home crowd, to not let the questions about when The Streak would end make it to the next spring training in Fort Lauderdale. His decision. His terms.

A different kind of history, three years and two weeks from when he had passed Gehrig. He sat down, but this was history that would stand forever. Somebody would beat McGwire someday, and Sosa. Someday, if Ken Griffey, Jr., stayed healthy and interested, he would break Henry Aaron's record of 755 lifetime homers. Maybe someday there would even be a hitter who could hit in 57 straight games and beat DiMaggio. There would never be another Ripken, no matter how long baseball is played. When Ripken sat down against the Yankees, the next-longest consecutive-game streak belonged to Albert Belle.

For the White Sox that afternoon, Belle had played in his 327th straight game.

So on this day, after all the home runs, after all the coverage McGwire and Sosa had gotten, Cal Ripken, Jr., made them move aside, made himself the story in baseball even on a day when McGwire hit No. 65 against the Brewers in Milwaukee, and would have had No. 66 if an umpire had not mistakenly ruled fan interference on another ball that made the seats in old County Stadium.

Ripken would lead the news and the sports reports on this night. Ripken would be on the front page of every newspaper in the country the next morning because he was in the dugout and Ryan Minor was playing third base for the Orioles. When the Yankees found out before the game that Ripken wasn't playing, they came as a group to the top step of their dugout at Camden Yards and applauded.

He won that World Series in '83. He was twice MVP of the American League. We knew early he was going to the Hall of Fame, and nothing he ever did for the Orioles changed anybody's mind. He had been blessed with talent and heart, he was stubborn and proud and built to last, like the hitting machine his father had restored for him. Managers came and went with the Orioles. Owners came and went. The Orioles moved from Memorial Stadium to Camden Yards. Ripken moved from short to third, and moved down in the batting order. He lost speed. He lost power. And he showed up to play every day, because if there was a game going on—any kind of game—how could he sit it out?

Now there were heroes all over baseball. Once he felt like the only hero, when baseball needed one most. McGwire carried baseball now, Sosa did, the Yankees did. A lot of people did in 1998. In another time, it seemed as if Ripken carried everybody.

Where were you when baseball really started to get up?

When Ripken passed Gehrig.

You could draw a straight line from No. 2,131 for Ripken through No. 62 for McGwire, right to No. 62 by Sammy Sosa.

And it was well worth remembering on the night before summer officially ended in '98. It was worth remembering as we looked at pictures of Ripken in the dugout while the Yankees–Orioles game was going on, shaking hands with the fans, signing baseballs for his teammates, mugging once in a while for the television cameras he had to know were trained on him all night long. Let the others be baseball heroes now. Baseball history wasn't made this night with a home run, with a mad scramble for the ball behind the outfield wall. It was made in the manager's office at Camden Yards by Cal Ripken, Jr., in somebody else's September.

No notes for the kids on this night.

You needed a book.

For weeks, ever since McGwire had hit No. 62, the replays of Roger Maris's 61st had been endless in Cable America, on ESPN and CNN and Fox and Classic Sports, all the places where you could find baseball on television. That day in October in '61, all I could remember was the voice of the great Yankee character and shortstop, Phil Rizzuto, known forever as the Scooter.

It was spontaneous and simple. Pure Scooter.

"Fastball hit deep to right . . . This could be it! . . . Holy Cow!"

Now in 1998, the calls of McGwire's home runs sounded as if they had been written out beforehand, rehearsed, even by great old broadcasters like Jack Buck, whose call on Kirk Gibson in the World Series once had come straight from the heart. On Fox, the night of

McGwire's 62nd, Buck's son Joe, working with Tim McCarver, did not have time for any scripted remarks because the ball got out of Busch Stadium so quickly. McGwire's vicious line drive barely made it over the left-field fence, and all Joe Buck could do was think and react and then do what all of us watching wanted to do, which was look at the pictures of McGwire, his delighted trip around the bases, and react ourselves, feel what we wanted to feel about all this without being told anything by anybody.

All the way down the stretch, announcers for the Cardinals and Cubs acted as if their calls would someday be a part of the history of the moment, the way Al Michaels's hockey call had been at the Lake Placid Olympics of 1980. It was the game between the United States and the USSR, and the United States wasn't supposed to have a chance. Then they had pulled off the upset of the century in Olympic sports, and the last seconds were ticking off the clock in the small rink in Lake Placid, and this is what Michaels, working the game for ABC Sports, yelled at the whole world:

"Do you believe in miracles? . . . YES!"

Now, in the home-run September, everybody wanted to be Michaels. Jack Buck, bless his heart, said something one night about a flight taking off for the Planet Maris. And so when you would hear the almost innocent wonder in Rizzuto's signature call—"Holy Cow!"—it brought back more innocent times in baseball.

Which is what the summer of '98 was all about for all those with baseball memories that involved more than stats, numbers pulled from the *Baseball Encyclopedia.*

Especially for sons who had become fathers.

On the last Saturday in September, I was channel-surfing with Zach. And there was Maris at the plate. I can't tell you the cable outlet or the show, just that I knew right away that it was once again that last Sunday of the '61 season.

I said to Zach, "Watch this."

"Who's that?"

"Roger Maris. Remember? He's the one whose record—"

He gave me The Look. He was better at it than his brothers had been at his age. But then, he had learned it from his brothers. How dare you give such obvious information to *me*, Zach Lupica.

Age six.

"—the record that McGwire broke. I *know*, Dad."

We both listened to Rizzuto's voice. He didn't sound much older than one of my kids. Calling the most famous home run in baseball history in a backyard voice.

Maris went around the bases, and then his teammates were shoving him up and out of the dugout at Yankee Stadium for what is supposed to have been the first official home-run curtain call in the history of the place.

"How come he didn't say what they say now?" Zach said.

"Who didn't say?"

"The announcer."

"Say what?"

He jumped up, because this is always a show with him, and gave me his very best John Sterling impression. When Sterling does his play-by-play of Yankee games on the radio, he has two signature calls of his own. One comes at the end of any game the Yankees win:

"The Yankees win! . . . Th-uh-uh-uh-uh-uh Yankees win!"

The other comes when Sterling is sure a ball a Yankee has hit is out of the park.

Zach did it now.

"It is high! . . . It is far! . . . It is . . . GONE!"

He looked at me.

"The man didn't do that."

"No," I said. "He did not."

The next day at Yankee Stadium, I was with Rizzuto, who had come to be a part of Joe DiMaggio Day, to present his old teammate with all the World Series rings that had been stolen from DiMaggio in the 1960s. I told Rizzuto, now retired as one of the Yankee broadcasters, that I had heard him again the day before, for about the hundredth time lately, making his call on Maris.

Bringing back the finale of my golden season.

Rizzuto was eighty-one in September of '98, but looked wonderful, tanned and energetic, so much younger than DiMaggio. And the high-pitched whine of a voice was still as young as it ever was, still part of the sound track of my own boyhood, everybody who was ever in range of that voice, on television or radio, for forty seasons that began after his retirement in the 1950s.

"You know, it's funny," he said. "I've been on the air more this September with that one call than I was a lot of Septembers I worked towards the end of my career."

He shook his head, mock disgust.

"I just wish I coulda come up with something a little better than 'Holy Cow,' " he said.

I told him that his call had always worked just fine for me, and just about everybody who had grown up with him the way I had.

"Boy, it seems like yesterday," Scooter Rizzuto said. "But hey, a lot of things do."

He looked down at the Balfour box he had in his hands, the one with the exact replicas of all the Series rings inside.

"I guess these are what you get for the guy like Joe D. who's got everything," Rizzuto said, then grinned and said, "In the old days, the only thing he wanted from me was to get on base."

He walked off with the rings, like a best man at a wedding, and went looking for Joe D. on another Sunday afternoon for them at the Stadium.

DIMAGGIO HAD BEEN HERE FOR THE FIRST DAY OF the regular season at Yankee Stadium; now he was here for the last, before the playoffs. The difference was dramatic. It was as if he had aged six years in the six months since April.

But at about 12:30 in the afternoon on Joe DiMaggio Day at Yankee Stadium, the first official Joe DiMaggio Day since the end of the 1949 season, he once again came out of the elevator at the basement level at the Stadium. Georgie, a member of the grounds crew, was waiting with a golf cart to drive him down to the Yankee clubhouse. They had never brought a cart for him before, not on any of the Opening Days. On the day that closed out the remarkable Yankee regular season, on the day when these Yankees would win their 114th game, they sent Georgie's white cart this time for DiMaggio. Everybody could see how tired he looked.

There were the two security men with him. There were a couple of photographers waiting for him, one television camera, a few print reporters. And me.

DiMaggio raised a hand and waved. Even that took effort. He smiled and said, "How's your sister?"

A yesterday for him, one that had always given us a small but meaningful connection.

DiMaggio used to spend part of the year at his sister's home in San Francisco, before almost all of his free time was limited to Fort Lauderdale. And when the weather was right, he would go for a walk along the water, near the St. Francis Yacht Club. It is one of the most beautiful spots in a beautiful city. My sister, Susan, and her husband lived right across from the yacht club, on Marina Boulevard. She was pregnant with her first child, but even late in the pregnancy, she would walk and jog slowly in the afternoon.

She was out one day and a guy on a bicycle lost control

and nearly ran her over. She didn't get knocked down, but it was close.

From behind her, she saw a hand, and heard a voice.

"Are you all right, young lady?"

She looked up and it was DiMaggio, dressed impeccably in his first-pitch clothes, blazer and shirt and tie and slacks.

She told him she was fine.

He shook his head.

"You could have been hurt."

She assured him she was fine, and introduced herself, saying, "I think you know my brother," and he said he did.

"Are you going to keep walking?" DiMaggio said.

Susan said she was.

"Would you like some company?"

She said that would be wonderful, and for the next forty-five minutes the two of them walked and talked along the water. She said DiMaggio could not have been more charming. She wasn't looking for an autograph. She didn't want to ask him baseball questions. She didn't want anything from DiMaggio except the company. They talked about New York and San Francisco and restaurants, and when they got back to where her house was, they shook hands.

"Let's do this again," he said.

They never did. But there had never been a time since when I had seen DiMaggio, either at the ballpark or at the offices of my paper, the *Daily News*—he would come to visit his friend Bill Gallo, the legendary sports cartoonist at the paper—when he did not ask about my sister, or mention that he had not been back to San Francisco lately. After all the columns I had written about him, after the time I had spent writing a piece for *Esquire* magazine in the early nineties, those few minutes with my sister one April afternoon along the water in San Francisco were my corner of DiMaggio's life, my entrée to him.

Now they were again, on his own Joe DiMaggio Day at the Stadium.

"I hardly get back there anymore," he said, meaning San Francisco.

I asked him how he was feeling.

"Old," he said.

He said Chicago had taken a lot out of him. He had been there the previous three days for a round of ceremonies. There had been a park named in his honor, some other appearances. He came out of San Francisco and New York and the Yankees claimed him as their own, but the season had been a celebration of all baseball things and so many old heroes, and so Chicago had decided to honor DiMaggio. And the highlight of the old man's week had been swinging a bat to ring the bell at the Chicago Commodities Exchange.

"They all stopped work and began to applaud," he said. "It went on for fifteen minutes. I felt as if millions of dollars were being lost."

No one cared at the Chicago Commodities Exchange. All summer long, the city had come to a stop every time Sammy Sosa came to the plate. Now it stopped to watch DiMaggio make one more swing.

"I put a pretty good dent in that bell," he said.

Georgie asked him now if he wanted to get into the cart, DiMaggio said he would walk, and Georgie drove on ahead of him. DiMaggio walked slowly and talked about the rings that Rizzuto was supposed to present to him. He showed his left hand.

"All these years, this is the only one I held on to, because it was on my hand when the others got stolen," he said.

"Which one is that?"

"The first one," DiMaggio said. "From '36."

He sighed and said almost the same thing Rizzuto had said about No. 61 from Maris.

"Don't ask me what I did yesterday," he said. "But the '36 Series seems like it was just the other day."

He came around the corner, and a couple of the clubhouse men came running to shake his hand and ask him if he needed anything. "A chair," DiMaggio said, and a folding chair appeared and DiMaggio sat down heavily and waited for the time when Georgie would drive him out to right field, where DiMaggio would get out of the golf cart and get into a white '56 Thunderbird convertible—because he had hit in 56 straight games once—and make one more victory lap around the Stadium.

The reporters caught up with him again and asked him if he had been following McGwire and Sosa, their amazing long-ball, long-distance theater.

"You bet I've followed them," he said. "Hasn't everyone?" Then he was telling the reporters about swinging the bat at the Chicago Commodities Exchange. And the dent he had put in that bell. And then he was talking about how times had changed in baseball, especially for home-run hitters, and what it had been like when he was young to try to hit a ball out of the old Yankee Stadium to either left or left center or dead center. In the reconfigured Stadium, there was a huge, colorful Getty sign way above left field, looking like the highest point in the park. Joe Torre liked to joke that in DiMaggio's day "Joe had to hit one over the Getty sign to get a home run to left."

Meaning he had to hit a ball halfway to Connecticut.

On this day, when McGwire would hit home runs 69 and 70 in St. Louis, punctuate the end of his season in that grand way, DiMaggio said, "I'd've liked to have gotten a crack at these balls the fellas are hitting nowadays," in a voice so soft the words seemed to run out of steam right in front of him.

He said, "And play in a few of these modern ballparks."

The old man was saying that maybe it would have been easier for him to dent a few more outfield seats the way he had dented that bell in Chicago.

Someone asked him whom he was rooting for, McGwire or Sosa, and he said he had been getting that question all the time.

"I'm rooting for both of them," he said.

A few of the Yankees poked their heads out the clubhouse door, like children, and came out to say hello to DiMaggio. David Wells was the first. He is the Yankee most in love with all the Yankee lore, and wanted to tell DiMaggio that he had come into possession of the last big-league uniform Babe Ruth had ever worn, in 1935, with the Boston Braves.

The sight of Wells, Wells's excitement about the uniform, made DiMaggio brighten.

"You said 1935?" he said to Wells.

Wells nodded.

"Before my time," Joe DiMaggio said.

Time for Georgie to drive him out to right field, into the sun and noise. He got into the convertible and Bob Sheppard, the Yankee public address announcer, began to read from a script about the man always identified here as "the greatest living ballplayer." Before the game, Sheppard had sat in the media dining room and I had asked when his voice had first become the voice of the Stadium.

"Nineteen fifty-one, Opening Day," he said. "Joe's last season was my first."

Then, without being asked, Sheppard had gone through the Yankee batting order from that April afternoon forty-seven years before.

Like it was yesterday.

The ballpark full of yesterdays on Joe DiMaggio Day, always full of ghosts.

These ghosts now, from Sheppard:

LF—Jackie Jensen
SS—Phil Rizzuto
RF—Mickey Mantle
CF—Joe DiMaggio
C—Yogi Berra
1B—Johnny Mize
3B—Billy Johnson
2B—Jerry Coleman
P—Vic Raschi

"The Yankees won, five to nothing," Sheppard said.

Now, his voice ringing over the day and the pictures on the giant screen in the outfield, Sheppard spoke once more of DiMaggio's career, his greatest accomplishments, his mystique. The white convertible made its way slowly across the outfield, right to center to left, DiMaggio making his familiar Royal Family wave while the background music was Simon and Garfunkel singing "Mrs. Robinson." Joe DiMaggio hadn't gone anywhere, he was still here. Then the Yankee Stadium organist, Eddie Layton, played "Thanks for the Memories."

The ballpark heard Bob Sheppard say that DiMaggio had "exemplified and encapsulated the spirit of baseball as we have come to know it."

Sheppard: "He illuminated Yankee Stadium with grace, elegance, and sheer presence."

Finally, the car made its way to home plate. There was a presentation from Major League Baseball and a reading of a proclamation from the mayor about this officially being Joe DiMaggio Day in New York City. DiMaggio did not speak. There was some hesitation near the end, and then Rizzuto, sensing that DiMaggio was about to walk off, thinking the ceremonies had concluded, came bouncing out of the Yankee dugout before Sheppard even introduced him, as if he were racing out from shortstop to catch some short fly ball before DiMaggio had to come in from center. The people in the stands exploded before they ever heard Rizzuto's name. Yankee fans know their own.

And for a few moments at the end of the season, the kind of splendid season they both once knew in this place, on this field, DiMaggio and Rizzuto, center fielder and shortstop, stood together in the sun. They had played glamour positions on great Yankee teams. Rizzuto batting second, playing short, on that '51 team Bob Sheppard remembered, DiMaggio playing center, batting cleanup. In a few minutes, Derek Jeter would play short, bat second for the Yankees on the day when they would go to 114–48. Bernie Williams would play center, bat cleanup. You wondered if someday, when Jeter and Williams were in their eighties, they would come back and be together for one more moment in the sun like this, if old Yankees, old Yankee memories, would be as important in the next baseball century as they had been all across this one.

Old boys of summer.

They finally waved goodbye and walked off the field together, made their way slowly and carefully down the dugout steps, walked up the carpeted runway toward the clubhouse. Rizzuto shook DiMaggio's hand.

Then suddenly, as if on impulse, the little man embraced DiMaggio. The gesture seemed to surprise Rizzuto as much as it did DiMaggio.

"You take care of yourself," Rizzuto said.

DiMaggio nodded.

"I'll see you at the World Series," Joe DiMaggio said.

SIX MONTHS FROM WHEN MY SONS AND I HAD GONE to Roger Dean Stadium in Jupiter to see Mark McGwire play a spring game against the Tampa Bay Devil Rays, the Yankees beat the Devil

Rays, 8–3. Williams, the new Yankee center fielder, the successor out there to DiMaggio and Mantle, went 2-for-2 and won the American League batting championship. Jeter went 1-for-4 to finish with an average of .324, the best season any Yankee shortstop had had since Scooter Rizzuto was Most Valuable Player in the league in '50. A kid named Shane Spencer hit his third grand slam in nine days. Spencer had been so hot in September that the day before, you had looked out to the scoreboard at the Stadium and seen this:

McGwire: 68

Sosa: 66

Spencer: 9

Across the country from Yankee Stadium, in St. Louis, a million miles from Jupiter in the spring, thirty-seven years after Maris had hit No. 61 off Tracy Stallard of the Red Sox, Mark McGwire hit No. 69 against Mike Thurman of the Expos.

Before he hit No. 70 against a right-handed pitcher named Carl Pavano.

Scooter Rizzuto had it exactly right after all, on this same kind of baseball day thirty-seven years before.

Holy Cow.

With three games left in the season, McGwire and Sosa were tied with 65 home runs. Since McGwire had broken Roger Maris's record on September 8, Sosa had hit seven home runs and McGwire had hit three. One last time, they were tied.

And somehow all of us who had watched and cared knew they weren't done yet, that a story like this needed a last act worthy of everything that had come before.

On Friday night, McGwire facing the Expos in St. Louis and

Sosa playing in the Astrodome in Houston against the Astros, Sosa hit No. 66, off pitcher Jose Lima. An 0–1 count. Top of the fourth. When the word of it reached the scoreboard at Busch Stadium, there was the kind of sudden quiet you get in a ballpark sometimes, when a day or night in baseball goes wrong. The quiet I remember best is October 2, 1978, Fenway Park, the Yankees against the Red Sox in that one-game playoff for the American League East. Bucky Dent's home run hit the screen above the Green Monster in left field and suddenly it seemed the only thing you could hear in Fenway were the shouts from the Yankees as they came out of the dugout to greet Dent. Other than that, the place was as still as the baseball winter.

Then the crowd roused itself and cheered even louder for McGwire than it had at the start of the Cardinals–Expos game. All along, in St. Louis more than anywhere else, they had been sure that their man would finish first. They were more sure than ever the night McGwire passed Maris. No one in the ballpark could believe that the eighth of September would end up a footnote to Sammy Sosa's home-run title, Sosa's season.

It would be the last time anybody would pass McGwire in the '98 baseball season, maybe for a very long time. And maybe forever.

Sosa was at 66 and McGwire was at 65 for about forty-five minutes on the last Friday night of the regular season. He was after Sosa now the way Sosa had been after him since June, and in the fifth inning, against Shayne Bennett, McGwire hit his own No. 66. He stood in the on-deck circle the way he always had, all the way back to Roger Dean Stadium in the spring, eyes closed, barrel of his bat on his right shoulder. No practice swings. He would just close his eyes and focus on this one at bat.

See the ball over the fence before he hit it over the wall, usually in left.

He did it again.

They were tied again.

Never a season like this, never in your life.

"He never talked about it much, either publicly or privately," Tony La Russa would say when it was over. "He knew he had this concentration device to call on, and he had a lot of confidence that he would be able to tune out all the extraneous information and focus on the at bat, times four. Every game. It was a tremendous comfort for him. He just knew he had this marriage of terrific physical power and the power of his mind.

"Listen, he knew, okay? Looking back at his fifty-two home runs two seasons ago, the fifty-eight last season, he could see that sixty-two was possible. He knew he had something special going. And he had generated a confidence that he could pull this off. A big key was staying healthy. In the end, it all came down to getting the at bats."

Only a handful of at bats now, two games left. Two games, times those four at bats a game, maybe five if the Cardinals were really scoring runs.

All the way from the last night of March and that grand slam against Ramon Martinez to here.

On Saturday afternoon against the Expos, McGwire hit two more, the first against Dustin Hermanson, the next against Kirk Bullinger.

Now he had 68.

La Russa went up to him in the clubhouse and asked how much he had left.

"One last game," Mark McGwire said.

La Russa: "He had primed himself to play through Sunday."

He hit two more on Sunday and got to 70. The last against Pavano. Bottom of the seventh. Bottom of his season. Two men on. Another line drive to left. And then McGwire was done.

There is the feeling that if you went out to Busch Stadium in November, or December, or in the middle of January, they would still

be there, still holding on to the last Sunday, September 27, still standing and cheering McGwire.

"To say the least, I amazed myself," McGwire said that day in St.
Louis. "I am absolutely exhausted. I don't think you can use your
mind any more than I did playing this game of baseball. I've amazed
myself that I've stayed in the tunnel for so long."

Saying these things now in the light of what he had done.

"Number seventy almost felt like sixty-two," he said. "The
crowd, the players on the Expos shaking my hand . . . I mean, it's
just . . . What can I say? I'm speechless, really."

They asked McGwire what they had always asked Ruth, and
then Maris after him: Would somebody ever break this record?

"Will it be broken someday?" McGwire said. "Could be. Will I
be alive? Possibly."

In the Cardinals' clubhouse that day, La Russa said he sought out
Jack Buck.

"What this guy did and the way he did it, well, I always felt in-
adequate trying to describe it," La Russa said. "And I mentioned
that to Jack, who is the most eloquent guy I know."

The old man, who had stayed around baseball long enough to
see this, to be talking about McGwire on the radio while his son, Joe
Buck, did the same on television, smiled at Tony La Russa.

"You can't describe it," Buck said.

Sometimes there are no words when you cannot believe what
you just saw.

MY SONS AND I WATCHED ALL THE REPLAYS OF
Nos. 69 and 70 and watched them again. And watched the clips from
McGwire's press conference after the game, and watched him on the
field for the final ceremonies of the summer in St. Louis.

Watched him stand on the field and wave goodbye.

When the boys were asleep, with a football game on the television now, the phone rang.

My dad.

"I waited until I figured the boys were asleep," he said.

He wanted to talk about the end of it.

So we did. We talked all about McGwire hitting five home runs the last three days of the season. I told him about being with DiMaggio earlier in the afternoon at the Stadium, told him about DiMaggio's ride in the T-Bird, and about the rings, about how exhausted Joe looked until he got out on the field and stood next to Rizzuto.

Then I told him about watching 69 and 70 after the boys' soccer games.

"It's a good number, seventy," Bene Lupica said finally. "Sixty was always a better number than sixty-one."

He had been born three years before Babe Ruth hit 60. He was seventeen the year DiMaggio hit in 56 straight games. He married my mother the year before DiMaggio played his last game for the Yankees. I had first loved baseball watching Maris with him. My sons first loved baseball watching McGwire with both of us.

"It was a pretty good summer, Pop," I said.

"They all are," my father said.

He had passed a summer like this on to me once.

Now I had done the same to my sons.

In September...

The Yankees won their division with a record of 114–48. The Indians won the Central with 89–73, a full 25 games behind the Yankees. The Rangers won the West at 88–74.

In the National League, the winners were the Braves (106–56), the Astros (102–60), and the Padres (98–64).

In addition to everything else, we ended up with three 100-win teams.

McGWIRE GOT HIS 70, KNOCKED IN 147 RUNS. Sosa *ended up with 66 home runs, 158 RBIs.*

Ken Griffey, Jr., was treated as some kind of afterthought after McGwire and Sosa pulled away from him and Griffey ended up with 56 homers, 146 RBIs, 387 total bases, a slugging percentage of .611. The White Sox's Albert Belle hit .328, had 49 homers, drove in 152, had 99 extra-base hits, 399 total bases, a slugging percentage of .655. And Belle got lost, too.

Another amazing afterthought at the end of the summer of '98.

Bernie Williams won the American League batting championship. Larry Walker of the Colorado Rockies won the National League batting championship at .363. Tom Glavine of the Braves would win his second Cy Young Award, just because there seems to be a rule that someone from the Braves—Glavine or Greg Maddux or John Smoltz—always wins the Cy Young. Rickey Henderson stole 66 bases for the A's at the age of thirty-nine. Greg Vaughn, who had failed a Yankee physical when the Yankees tried to trade for him during the '97 season, hit 50 home runs for the Padres. Four players in each league got to 200 hits: Dante Bichette of the Rockies, Vinny Castilla of the Rockies, Craig Biggio of the Astros, and Vladimir Guerrero of the Expos in the National League; Alex Rodriguez, Mo Vaughn, Derek Jeter, Belle in the American.

Eric Davis, recovering cancer patient, did indeed have his 30-game hitting streak for the Orioles, longest in the majors.

Eric Davis would indeed be Comeback Player of the Year in the American League.

And, in September, there would be one more comeback to touch everyone's heart. Especially mine.

It came from Jim Abbott, the remarkable left-hander who had been born without a right hand, and who had never let that stop him for a day in baseball. He had gone to the University of Michigan on a baseball scholarship, pitched for the United States in the Olympics in Seoul, South Korea, in 1988, and gone straight to the big leagues with the Angels.

Then he ended up with the Yankees and pitched that no-hitter one September Saturday while Chris and Alex and I listened in the car, then we went straight to Bob's Sports and bought Yankee caps in honor of Abbott.

By 1996 Jim Abbott was back with the Angels, but it was as if all the years of beating the world one-handed had taken too much out of his left arm. He was 2–18 that year. His earned run average was 7.48. The next year, he was out of baseball. And I thought, okay. He could walk away without regrets, even if he was still just thirty.

His name was right there on the first page of one of my Baseball Encyclopedias, *in lights forever, the kid from Flint, Michigan, whose right arm quit at the wrist and who had surprised and thrilled us all. If somebody had told me the first time I'd met him that he would have exactly the career he did have, I would have cheered.*

But Abbott doesn't quit very easily. The White Sox gave him one last chance. He took it. He went to the minors at the age of thirty. He learned to pitch all over again, without as much hard stuff this time. Moving the ball around. More sleight of hand, one-handed. He started to feel good about himself again. He started to look good. And by September, he was back in the big leagues.

And on September 5, 1998, five years and one day from when he threw his no-hitter for the Yankees, he faced the Yankees in Comiskey Park. I told all the Lupica boys they had to watch for at least a little while. So they could draw a line in memory from the no-hitter to this comeback for Jim Abbott.

"He's your friend, right, Dad?" Chris said. "You met him when he was in high school, right?"

"Twelve years ago," I told them all. "He's one of the guys I feel like I saw first."

Abbott was shaky that night in the first inning. Paul O'Neill doubled in a run, scored on a Bernie Williams single. But then the White Sox gave Abbott a lead, and he settled right down, and when he finally left with the lead in the seventh, he was on his way to the victory, on his way to a marvelous 5–0 record for the White Sox. When he was asked about the ovation afterward, what he felt about it, Abbott said, "Gratitude and humility. There were points where I didn't know if I'd ever play again, so these are thrills I thought had passed."

That night, long after the boys were in bed, the thrill was mine. I watched him walk off the mound and wave, and it was as if he was waving away the twelve years. And it was that day in Flint in '86, and he was a skinny teenaged kid pounding his Rawlings glove with his left hand and talking about how he had been 10–3 at Flint Central his senior year, with a 0.76 earned run average, striking out 148 batters in 73 innings. How he had played quarterback on the football team.

Oh, and by the way, how he had batted .427 as a senior, with seven homers.

Then it was time for that game of catch, so I could see how he threw and got the glove on, then off, so he could throw again. He was about thirty yards away, and after a few minutes the ball was beginning to make bigger and bigger popping noises in the glove he had given me, and I was just making sure that I paid attention to the ball and not to whatever Abbott was doing with that glove switch or the ball was going to hit me right between the eyes.

I wrote at the time: "I wanted to remember this game of catch, because I began to feel strongly that it would be important someday that I knew Jim Abbott when."

Never more important than now. . . .

· *eight* ·

October

THE SEASON IS SUPPOSED TO BEGIN IN APRIL. THE postseason is supposed to begin in October. So one more trick of the calendar now at Yankee Stadium, on September 30, the Yankees a few hours away from their second playoff game, against the Texas Rangers, having already won the first game, 2–0, behind David Wells. It was officially October in baseball. After 114 victories in the regular season, the Yankees were 1–0 in the October season. McGwire sat down now, until next spring. Sosa would soon be out of the playoffs in three straight games against the Atlanta Braves, without hitting another home run.

The Yankees were up.

They were supposed to close as hard as McGwire had, show the same finishing kick. More than any of the other teams left, they would be the last high drama of the golden season. Win or lose. They would get to 125 victories—three in the first round, four in the American League Championship Series, four more in the World Series—and finish what would be called the greatest single season in baseball history, perhaps professional sports history. Or they would be remembered the way the Indians of '54 were remembered, as a team that fell apart in the stretch. The Indians won their 111 games in '54, then got swept in four games in the Series by Willie Mays and the New York Giants.

"Where else," Derek Jeter had said two days before, before Game 1 against the Rangers, "would you want to be in October except here?"

On nights like this, Yankee Stadium didn't just feel like the best baseball place, it felt like the only place, from the time you came down from the subway platform beyond the outfield walls, from the time you got out of your car; from the time the Yankees came out of the parking lot and the visiting players got off the bus.

Just not for everyone, not on this particular night.

At a little after five, Darryl Strawberry was headed out of the Stadium, walking the blue line away from the clubhouse, walking it past Joe Torre's office, walking it right toward the stairway across from the media dining room, walking away from the baseball night when he should have been walking right into the middle of it. Strawberry wore a white warm-up suit and expensive high-top leather basketball sneakers and carried the small leather bag for his cell phone in his big left hand. He tried to look relaxed when I came down the stairs and saw him there talking quietly to a radio reporter. He leaned against the wall and made a gesture that said give him a minute. But there was something wrong, and it showed. This is the kind of face everybody gets when there is something not quite right in a hospital test, a shadow on a test result the doctors do not like and cannot immediately explain.

This was a waiting-room fact underneath Yankee Stadium, at a time when the rest of the place waited for the first game of the playoffs.

The pains in his stomach—it was just a moment in the green room that day at HBO, a note I had taken and promptly forgotten, the mention of cramps one Sunday in the clubhouse—had not gone away and finally had sent Strawberry to the hospital for tests. And now there would be more tests tomorrow, a lot more tests. Just like that, Strawberry was out of Game 1 of the Rangers series, maybe out of the whole season, depending on what the new tests showed.

October would begin for him at a New York hospital just a few minutes from the ballpark, Columbia Presbyterian.

"It's always something with me, isn't it?" he said when the radio reporter moved on.

Without the pains in his stomach that had been bothering him for almost two months, there would have been only this question for Strawberry with a right-handed pitcher—Rick Helling—starting for the Rangers: Is Darryl the starting left fielder or is he the designated hitter? The Yankees had scored only two runs in the first game, might need more tonight behind Andy Pettitte, who hadn't pitched very well in September. But now there were other questions. Doctor questions. For the first time the suggestion had been raised that he might have cancer.

All the doctors were saying for now was that there was an infection in his colon. And right away, Strawberry thought about Eric Davis. Boyhood friend. Baltimore Oriole. Survivor of colon cancer. Now almost certainly the Comeback Player of the Year in the American League. Around doctors and hospitals, you always fear the worst, no matter who you are. You worry that there might be some time bomb inside you even if the Lord gave you a body built for baseball and sports like Strawberry's. As soon as they talked about the infection being in the colon, as soon as the first doctor talked about a possible "mass" in there, Strawberry started thinking about Davis and what he had been through, and could not stop thinking about him.

"It can't be," he told his wife the night before. "What would be the odds of me and Eric getting the same kind of cancer?"

Now, maybe a hundred feet from the Yankee clubhouse, Strawberry explained what the doctors had seen as a "dark area."

Dan Quisenberry, the retired relief pitcher who had owned the month of October in 1985, along with the rest of the Kansas City Royals, had just died after his own long fight with brain cancer. Quisenberry was just forty-five. Strawberry's mother, Ruby, had died of cancer a couple of years before.

And there was Davis.

What were the odds?

"I'm pretty comfortable now that it's not cancer," Strawberry said. "But anytime there's something wrong inside your body and they don't know what it is, you're going to get spooked."

His face, the waiting-room face, told you he wasn't comfortable with any of this, that he hadn't ruled anything out. He was fidgeting now, edgy, the way he used to be as a kid when he was tired of talking to you, wanting to get out of here, not wanting to talk to anybody else. Get into his black Jeep and drive home to Charisse in New Jersey. He kept moving the leather bag from one hand to the other.

"You never worry when it's something baseball-related," he said. "A knee, something like that . . ."

The words died a few feet in front of him, as if he could step right over them on his way to the parking lot.

"I've been thinking all season about going deep in the playoffs," he said.

Then he talked about Davis again. About how both of them had been through so much since South Central L.A. Strawberry kept finding himself out of baseball. Davis retired for a year because he thought there had been too many injuries, too much wear and tear on the body with which he'd been blessed. Then he came back the way he did from cancer, as if he were young again. Without the pains in his stomach the last month of the season, Darryl probably would have been the Yankee leader in home runs.

"What happened to Eric would scare anybody," he said.

Out in the dugout, Joe Torre was talking about how cancer is the one thing you always fear when the tests come back wrong. "Cancer always comes to mind," Torre said. And maybe it was in Strawberry's mind all along, all the mornings when the pain was there as soon as he opened his eyes. For a while, it subsided as the game got closer; he joked that maybe adrenaline made it disappear. Then it would not subside. Then the ache was constant, worse than anything he felt in his creaky knees. The Yankees kept going. He would still get his swings, though not as many as before. There was some question near the end of September as to whether he would even make the playoff roster—his bat looks slow, you heard—and then there he was on the last weekend of the regular season, ripping a ball into the outfield, legging it into a double, standing there on second base, smiling, saying to Torre and everybody, I'm still here.

Now he was nowhere, caught between the ballpark and the hospital, not in the season but not out of it yet, his day ending at Yankee Stadium when it should have been beginning.

"I'll be fine," he said, and then headed up the steps to the parking lot.

The Yankees won again.

It was announced the next afternoon that Strawberry was suffering from colon cancer.

178 • Mike Lupica

S H A N E   S P E N C E R   W A S   T H E   O N E   W H O   W E N T   D E E P
against the Rangers.

The Yankees lost Strawberry's bat in a sudden, shocking way.
Cancer. The same cancer his best friend had gotten. But they had
Spencer's bat now. That is the way it has always worked in baseball.
Somebody steps out of the line, somebody moves in. By now, every-
one knew Strawberry's name. A few months before, no one had re-
ally known Spencer's, at least not the first time the Yankees called him
up from their Triple-A team in Columbus, Spencer replacing Chili
Davis when Davis hurt his ankle in April. Now everyone knew Shane
Spencer's baseball-hero name, a face that reminded you of a young
Mantle, knew that Spencer had hit ten home runs for the Yankees in
just 67 at bats, had hit three grand-slam home runs the last ten days
of the regular season.

In the history of the New York Yankees, seven players had hit
three grand-slam homers in one season:

Ruth.

Gehrig.

DiMaggio.

Don Mattingly.

Tommy Henrich.

Mike Stanley.

Shane Spencer.

He had played nine years in the minors. He came out of El
Cajon, California, and his parents now lived in a town called Shirley,
Arkansas, which Spencer described one day as a "yield sign with
some stores around it." He had never been a phenom of the Yankee
system, a player to watch, for a single day of his career. Then the
Yankees called him up. Sent him back down. Called him back up a
few more times and finally, in September, on a team headed for 114

wins, Spencer became a September star, Spencer became a sudden hitting sensation, Spencer is the one who made the home crowds go mad every time he came to the plate.

One day he said what his manager, Torre, would later say about him in October:

"If this is a dream, don't anybody wake me."

There was a time when it seemed that the best possible happy ending to his improbable story was when he made the Yankee post-season roster: guy out of nowhere getting his ticket punched all the way to October. But Shane Spencer, twenty-six years old, a phenom at last, wanted more. He'd had a little taste now. He'd heard what the Stadium sounded like when they were cheering for you, when they wanted you to make one of those home-run curtain calls that had begun with Maris in '61.

"This will only be a storybook if it has the right ending," he said.

Now in October, the front pages of the papers were filled with stories about Strawberry and his cancer and his impending surgery. The back of the paper was about Spencer hitting the home runs Strawberry had dreamed about hitting in the playoffs. Two years earlier, Strawberry had his own storybook ending in October, coming all the way back and hitting home runs and even making important plays in the field and winning another World Series in New York.

Spencer this time.

Two years before, the medical drama for the Yankees had been Torre's brother, Frank, waiting at Columbia Presbyterian for a heart transplant, finally getting a new heart the day before the Yankees closed out the Braves by winning Game 6 of the Series. In October of '98, Strawberry was in the same hospital watching Spencer, in the first postseason at bat of his life, take a Rick Helling pitch over the wall in left center at Yankee Stadium and nearly all the way to Mantle's plaque in Monument Park.

In Game 3 in Texas two nights later, on the night when the Yankees finished sweeping the Rangers, Spencer hit another home run, this one good for three runs. "I can't believe this is happening to me," Spencer said. The Yankees would score just nine runs in their three-game series against the Rangers. Shane Spencer knocked in four of them with his two home runs.

Who could make up a story like this?

A season like this?

What were the odds?

"We're all in awe right now," David Cone said. "It's like we're watching a cult hero. Shane gets a bigger ovation than any of us."

"Short swing with some lift in it," a National League scout following the Yankees said. "No kidding, right now it looks a little bit like McGwire's."

"Personally," Paul O'Neill said, "I hope this kid hits a hundred home runs."

The day before Strawberry went into the hospital for his surgery, I talked to him on the telephone. He did not want to talk about the cancer. He wanted to talk about the Yankees, about the game the night before. About baseball.

Even about Spencer.

"You watch that guy [Spencer]," Darryl said, "and you have to smile."

He had put his bat down for now; Spencer had picked it up. He got off the blue line, and somebody else moved up at the Stadium. Spencer hits his home run with Darryl Strawberry's No. 39 stitched into his navy cap, same as the rest of the Yankees.

S TRAWBERRY'S SURGERY WAS SCHEDULED FOR S AT - urday, October 3. This was the Thursday night before that, between Games 2 and 3 of the Yankees–Rangers series.

The boys knew something was up, and now after dinner that

night, before we watched one of the other playoff games, I sat them down in the game-watching room.

"Remember I told you the other night that Darryl might be a little sick?" I said.

Nods.

"Well, it turns out it's a little more serious than he thought the first day."

"Does he have to have an operation?" Zach said.

Zach was two when he had a double-hernia operation. You can barely see the scar anymore, but he will still pull up his shirt and show it proudly, and without much urging. It is something he has that his brothers don't. When it comes to operations, he is the veteran in the family. The youngest getting to feel like the oldest for a change.

"Actually, he does," I said. "It turns out that he has cancer."

"What kind?"

Chris.

"Colon cancer. It's a pretty crazy coincidence—"

"Eric Davis had colon cancer," Chris said.

Of course. They know everything.

"That's right," I said. "He did. And you know, he's having one of the best seasons he ever had in his life."

"A thirty-game hitting streak," Chris said.

"He went to the hospital and they gave him these treatments last year, and he was back playing even before the season was over," I said. "Remember when Darryl was at my show, he was talking about how happy he was for Eric, how well he was doing?"

Chris said, "Darryl will be fine."

He is the one who makes all calamities disappear simply by changing the subject, and he did that now, because the game was about to come on.

Alex hadn't said anything and didn't say anything until I put him down to sleep that night. Alex prays every night, alternating the Our Father with the Beatitudes ("Blessed are the poor in spirit . . ."). Tonight he asked if it was all right to pray for Darryl, and I told him it was. And he did.

When he finished he rolled over on his back. Up on his ceiling are stars that he and my wife had pasted up there once, ones that give off a slight glow when he shuts off the lights. They have always seemed to fit Alex's world. He looked at the stars now, his hands clasped behind his head, and then he said to me, "Is Darryl going to die, Dad?"

You do not bluff Alex when he asks you straight-up like this. You do not even try to give him the dodge. Calamities do not disappear so easily for him. He is the one who wants to know about death and dying, God and heaven, the depth of the ocean, the height of the real stars in the sky.

He wants to know why things are the way they are.

"I would tell you if I thought he was," I said. "But I don't think he is. The doctors say they caught this deal early, he's young and strong. His friend beat this cancer, and I believe Darryl will, too."

"Okay, then," he said.

I sat there with him for a few moments, rubbing his back.

"Darryl's my first friend to get cancer," he said.

"I'll be talking to him next week," I said. "I'll tell him you're praying for him."

When I came up later to make sure he was covered and kiss him in the night, I noticed he had rearranged some things around on his headboard, moved a few of his special things over to this side of the room. His Darryl card. His signed baseball from Darryl.

His friend.

ON SATURDAY NIGHT, WHEN THE OFFICE CALLED to tell me the surgery was over for Darryl and the preliminary reports were that there had been no surprises, I left just one note, for Alex.

Allie Boy:
The doctors say everything went OK with Darryl's operation.
Your prayers must have helped.
Darryl sure is lucky to have a friend like you.
Dad.

Chris and Alex and Zach were waiting for me in the morning. Even though Game 2 between the Yankees and Indians had started at four in the afternoon, it had lasted nearly forever, and so all of them, youngest to oldest, were in bed when I finally got back from Yankee Stadium after eleven o'clock.

They had all watched the game, though.

They sure saw what happened.

Now it was as if they had come straight from the last out to breakfast. They were all talking at once, the breakfast table sounding like the bleachers at the Stadium again. All talking about the same play.

"Okay," I said. "Let me start off by asking everybody a question: What should Knoblauch have done?"

Three voices, same answer, because their mom had given it to them as she watched the game with them the night before.

"HE SHOULD HAVE GOTTEN THE BALL!"

The New York Yankees had won 118 games. If you counted the four playoff games they had won without a loss, the record for the season stood at 118–48 before yesterday's game. But in a 1–1 game against the Indians, in the top of the twelfth inning at Yankee Stadium, with the Indians' Enrique Wilson—running for Jim Thome—on first, Travis Fryman laid down a perfect sacrifice bunt. Tino

Martinez picked the ball up and threw to Chuck Knoblauch, over covering first. Fryman, running just inside the baseline, was between Martinez and Knoblauch, but Knoblauch never gave his first baseman the kind of target, way inside the base, that infielders are taught to give on plays like this, whether the base runner is on the line or inside it.

Suddenly the ball was hitting Travis Fryman in the back, and then it was past Knoblauch and rolling behind him.

Not on the blue line leading to the Yankee clubhouse now for Knoblauch.

Just the white chalk line behind first base at the Stadium.

Knoblauch looked at home-plate umpire Ted Hendry and pointed vaguely at where Fryman had been, saying that he had been interfered with. And some people—especially former umpire Steve Palermo, who happened to be a guest of NBC's Bob Costas in the NBC broadcast booth—agreed with Knoblauch that Fryman should have been called out, that he ran out of the baseline from the moment he put his bat on the ball and the ball hit the ground at the Stadium like a pillow hitting a bed.

Only, the umpires on the field did not agree with Knoblauch.

Enrique Wilson had never stopped running.

By the time Knoblauch went after the ball, threw it in desperation toward home plate, it was 2–1 Indians, on the way to being 4–1 Indians.

The Yankees had all those wins. They were 66 games over .500 for the season. For months they had been compared to the '72 Dolphins, who had finished with a 17–0 record, to Michael Jordan's 72–10 Chicago Bulls of 1995–96. Now, because the line between triumph and disaster in baseball is sometimes a baseline, the Yankees were even with the Indians, and facing three games at Jacobs Field in Cleveland, where the Indians had taken the Yankee season the October before this one.

From the start, this Yankee team had given you the class and teamwork and professionalism of the old Knick basketball teams of the late sixties and early seventies, the ones with Bill Bradley and Walt Frazier and Willis Reed and Earl Monroe and Dave DeBusschere. There had been six months and more of unforgettable baseball, now very much at risk because of a ball sitting there for a few seconds behind Knoblauch. The game would take four hours and twenty-eight minutes by the time it was over. It seemed the ball was behind Knoblauch at least that long.

Nobody had been close to the Yankees for months. They had swept the Rangers and won Game 1 from the Indians. But Fryman bunted and Knoblauch pointed and Wilson ran and the Yankees were even with the Indians.

In the year of the home run, this had all started with a ball that didn't travel fifty feet.

Knoblauch stood at his locker afterward and sounded like a fighter just waking up after being knocked cold.

"I just didn't know where the ball was," he said.

Someone wanted to know if he was embarrassed.

"I'm never embarrassed," he said. "Why would I be?"

The reporter asking the question said, "Well, failing this way."

Knoblauch said, "How did I fail?"

Down the hall, Travis Fryman, who started it all, said, "Ordinarily, you go get the ball, stop the runners, then argue the play."

In the 167th game of the Yankee season, after all that, we had been reminded of one more unchanging and enduring part of baseball: It is not just one player that can change everything, the way Piazza had with the Mets.

Sometimes all you need is one play.

Joe Torre would criticize the umpires, talking about how Fryman had never set foot inside the white chalk box that begins halfway to first base. George Steinbrenner would rage about the umpires stand-

186 · Mike Lupica

ing in the hallway between the home clubhouse and the visiting clubhouse, somehow turning the whole thing into an attack on American
League president Dr. Gene Budig. Some players would agree with
the umpires, that it was no call; other Yankees would say that Fryman
definitely should have been called out.

Knoblauch, for his part, was at least consistent in the Yankee
clubhouse, standing in front of his locker, just a few steps from the
manager's office. He kept saying the same things over and over, as if
trying to convince himself.

"I'd do the same thing again," he said.

He would get to Cleveland the next day and hold a press conference and give everybody the apology about the play they wanted
from him. But for now, this was a terrible moment for him, in what
had sometimes been a difficult first season for him in New York. He
had given the Yankees the leadoff man they needed, allowing Jeter
to hit second, setting up the whole batting order, the whole Yankee
offense. But Knoblauch had struggled with his throwing for most of
the season, even on routine throws from second base. And even
though he had hit 17 home runs and scored 117 runs, he had batted
just .265, after a lifetime batting average over .300 with the Twins.
Through it all, he and his family continued to deal with the ongoing
tragedy of his father, suffering from Alzheimer's disease: one family where there would be memories only for the son when the season
was over.

Now the son, in front of the whole country, had forgotten one
of the fundamental rules of sports: Don't stop playing until the play
is over.

Even Cliff McFeely's Ontarios knew that.

Across the Yankee clubhouse, Willie Randolph, the old Yankee
second baseman—twice a World Series champion at Knoblauch's
position—smiled and rubbed the top of his head. Randolph was the

Yankee third-base coach by now, and was sitting in the dugout when Fryman put the bunt down. He saw the bunt, the throw, the ball behind Knoblauch. Saw Knoblauch pointing instead of chasing.

Randolph jumped up so fast, yelling for Knoblauch to get the ball, he nearly knocked himself out on the dugout roof.

"As long as we win Friday [Game 3], this will all be forgotten," Randolph said. Another Yankee second baseman trying to convince himself of something.

But the Yankees lost Friday night in Cleveland. The Indians hit four home runs, one of them from Manny Ramirez of Washington Heights, and won Game 3. Now the Yankees were behind, two games to one.

After 118 wins, they needed one win.

Now.

ORLANDO (EL DUQUE) HERNANDEZ MADE EVERY-thing right for the Yankees.

He pitched the kind of game for the Yankees in Game 4 that he had once pitched for the Cuban national team, when he was the ace of that team, before being kicked off that team when officials of Fidel Castro's government suspected he was about to defect. He was forced to give up baseball completely, unless you counted softball sometimes on a weekend. He went to work as a therapist in a psychiatric hospital for a few dollars a day. And it was from there, from that kind of life in Cuba, from that form of baseball exile, that he had watched the October before as his half brother Livan had first pitched the Marlins past the Braves in the National League Championship Series, then past the Indians in the World Series.

Two months later, Orlando Hernandez defected from Cuba, in a boat in the night. There were seven other passengers with him, and they finally made it to the Caribbean island of Anguilla Cay. There was not just the danger of the trip; there was also the pain of leaving his two daughters behind with their mother and his mother in Havana. But this was his chance to be free; maybe there would be a way to free them later.

He was not just free from Castro; he was a free agent in baseball. He signed with the Yankees. He was either twenty-eight or thirty-two, depending on who was doing the talking. He started in the minors. He got his chance when Cone had to miss just the one start when his mother's dog bit him on the pitching hand. And then there was no stopping him. Then all the flair and showmanship and stuff came out of him. He would finish at 12–4, with a 3.13 earned run average. He was El Duque. Let everyone act surprised. He had always pitched like this, his whole life.

They asked him about the pressure of pitching against the Indians, a spot like this, maybe the great Yankee season on the line.

Asking someone who had made that trip from Cuba about pressure.

"I've pitched in three world championship games," he said. "I've pitched in the Olympics. I've pitched in national tournaments. I've pitched big games before."

He knew this was his biggest game. He had made the trip across the water to pitch a game like this, have a moment like this to himself. Have this kind of stage. At lunch on Saturday, seven hours before he would face the Indians and try to get the Yankees even in the series, Hernandez said, "People never miss an opportunity to ask why I left Cuba. They all ask. But they cannot understand it, really. The answer is here."

He tapped his chest, right over his heart.

The answer was there, and waiting for him at Jacobs Field. The trip that had begun the December before from Havana had brought him all the way there. He knew Castro would watch this game ("It makes me want to pitch better"). He knew his daughters would watch. The previous Sunday, he had been late for the Yankees' workout, and fined by Joe Torre. He had never explained his tardiness. But at lunch before Game 4 against the Indians, he said to a friend in Spanish, "I was talking to my daughters on the telephone. It was my only chance to speak to them. I was a father to my children again for those five minutes. I was doing what a man must do."

He went out against the Indians that night, and the only bad moment for him came in the first inning. The Yankees had scored a run in the top of the first, on a Paul O'Neill home run. But the Indians got two base runners against Hernandez, and then Jim Thome, who would end up with four home runs for the Indians in the American League Championship Series, came to the plate.

Hernandez threw him a high fastball and Thome hit it hard, and when the ball was first in the air, it seemed to be another home run for the Indians, to go with all the home runs the night before. Afterward, people would wonder how Hernandez and the Yankees would have reacted, how this game and this series and the Yankee season would have come out if Thome's ball had gone over O'Neill and over the right-field fence at Jacobs Field and the Indians had led the Yankees 3–1 in the first inning, the Indians trying to go ahead 3–1 in the series.

But not every ball went out of the park, not even in '98.

Thome had hit the ball toward the end of his bat. Maybe an inch from the sweet spot. An inch changing everything now. The ball hung in the air, and O'Neill got under it and caught it. The Yankees kept their lead. El Duque would pitch seven innings of shutout ball, giving the Indians the whole show, the high kicks, the spins, the fastballs. He struck out Ramirez in the sixth. He struck out Thome. The Yankees won, 4–0.

"I had no pressure, no fear," Hernandez said.

In the clubhouse afterward, he said, "I hope my daughters saw."

He had reached out for them with his great right hand. Fathers and daughters on this night, even with the daughters in another country, another world.

Fathers and daughters this time in baseball.

I WAS IN CLEVELAND WITH THE YANKEES. MY PARents were in Connecticut with my wife and the kids. So my father got to watch Games 3 and 4 and 5 of Yankees vs. Indians with three of his grandsons.

I called home after Game 4 and asked how the kids had liked the game.

"They loved it," he said. "The announcers started to tell about El Duque's trip out of Cuba and your boys know it by heart."

"They know everything, Pop," I said. "Where are they right now?"

"Out playing ball," he said. "Where else? Chris is using Alex's catcher's mitt and Alex is pitching. He's got his socks pulled up like El Duque."

When Alex wasn't watching the games, he was in uniform. Somebody's uniforms. He has more jerseys in those drawers under his bed than The Sports Authority. I could see him in the yard; he would have all of El Duque's moves down by now. The leg in the air, the turn of the head. Everything. The way he had Sosa down.

Over the phone, I said to my father, "Did they make you leave them notes?"

He laughed.

"They said yours are better," he said.

Thirty-seven years since he had written his last baseball note in the night. He was just out of practice.

The day before the first game of the 1998 World Series, a father and his teenaged son walked the path that first takes you past the retired numbers on the blue wall at the front of Monument Park at Yankee Stadium and then finally into what feels like the main room out there, to the place where you find the monuments for Babe Ruth and Miller Huggins and Lou Gehrig.

Neither father nor son had ever been to Yankee Stadium before. So they were like all the tourists and all the fans who had ever walked this path, into what feels like some magic garden. What better way to get ready for the thirty-fifth World Series at the Stadium than this sort of walking tour, one that began in the twenties with Ruth and Huggins and brought you all the way to this afternoon in October of '98?

"I didn't even know these were here," the father said, pointing toward the numbers on the wall.

The boy, just sixteen, looked somewhat bored, as if he were humoring his father, trying to share his excitement for all this history, close enough to touch. Not angels in the outfield at Yankee Stadium, just the usual ghosts. The father would joke later that the son would have found the trip to Monument Park more interesting if there had been something about Michael Jordan out behind the left-center-field wall.

"I had to see this," the father would say later. "And I wanted him to see it with me."

The father was Tony Gwynn, whose Padres had upset the Houston Astros and upset the Atlanta Braves and now would face the Yankees in the Series. After 2,928 hits in the big leagues, all of them with the Padres, after eight batting championships, Gwynn was back in the Series for the first time since 1984.

Better yet, he was at Yankee Stadium for the first time.

He had never played here, never attended a game here, never visited here.

When he came to New York for a three-game series against the Mets, he would be at Shea Stadium, that was it. He was too busy for sight-seeing. His workday starts earlier than anybody else's, at home or on the road, early in the afternoon at the batting cage, the ballpark empty except for the sweet sound of the line drives coming off his bat.

But now here he was at the Stadium, Anthony Gwynn II at his side, standing in front of Ruth's monument at the Stadium. He stood there the way my father had stood out here three years earlier and looked at Joe DiMaggio's plaque.

"Babe Ruth," Gwynn said softly.

He whistled now as softly as the words, and said, "Oh, man."

The Padres had won the first three games of the National League Championship Series, and finally beat the Braves in six games. The Yankees won the last three games of the American League Championship Series, not losing again after El Duque got the ball to start Game 4. So the splendid season would end not with the Yankees against the Braves, 114 wins against 106, as everyone had expected, a rematch of the '96 Series. The season would end with Yankees vs. Padres instead.

A team with all the World Series history against a team with hardly any.

The only other time the Padres had played in the Series, in '84, they had been able to get just one game off the Detroit Tigers. "I was a kid," Gwynn said. "I thought, 'Okay, we lost, but I'll get plenty of chances.' Little did I know." Now he was back, after fourteen seasons, so many of them spent on Padres teams that had no chance. He was back and he was finally on the inside at Yankee Stadium, better late than never. All across his career, he'd said that if he made it back to the Series, he wanted to do it with the Padres. He was from San Diego and San Diego State. The city was home, the team was home, all he had ever known in baseball. He wanted to go the distance with one team the way Gehrig had, DiMaggio, Mantle, Berra. Be that kind of baseball immortal.

There was a camera crew from ESPN following him out to Monument Park. But this was no show with Tony Gywnn. This was between him and baseball. Somehow, this is the way it is for everyone their first time out here, walking this path, seeing these sights. My father stood in center and said, "DiMaggio." Paul O'Neill still stands in right and thinks, Babe Ruth.

Gwynn went and stood in the open area where they will put the monument to DiMaggio someday, when he is gone.

The Series would begin with Kevin Brown of the Padres facing David Wells. And in Game 1 of his first World Series in fourteen years, in the first game he had ever played in Yankee Stadium, Tony Gwynn—one of the most famous singles hitters of all time— would bounce a Wells pitch off the facing of the upper deck in right field.

But the Series had really begun for him the day before, Gwynn out with ghosts of old-timers, feeling young. When it was over, someone asked if it was as good as he thought it would be, and Gwynn said, "It was better."

What was it Yogi said more than a half century before, when he came down from his submarine base in Connecticut?

A big, beautiful place for baseball. . . .

JOE DIMAGGIO WAS SUPPOSED TO THROW OUT THE first ball before Game 1.

"I'll see you at the World Series," he had told Phil Rizzuto less than a month before. Only now it came out that he was in a hospital in Florida, suffering from pneumonia. That is what we were told at the time, anyway.

It was only later that we would find out DiMaggio was sicker than that, much sicker.

Major League Baseball and the Yankees came up with a sensational substitute, even if the pinch hitter would only be asked to make a throw: Sammy Sosa. One last time, one last ballpark, he would smile and touch his heart and blow a kiss and wave to the crowd and be thanked for the home-run summer. At the end of the season, Sosa would have a curtain call at Yankee Stadium.

But first, all the years after riding the bus to his tryout with the Rangers, there would be a long, slow ride through lower Manhattan in New York City, in a parade that was all about him.

It was a Saturday, not a workday, in Manhattan. Wall Street was closed. So there would not be millions on the street, the way there are when the Yankees win the World Series; there would not be a blizzard of shredded computer printouts—replacing ticker tape—in the New York place known as the Canyon of Heroes. The Dominicans had wanted the parade in Washington Heights, but the mayor, Ruddy Giuliani, said no. Giuliani is famous in New York for being the kind of fanatic micromanager Steinbrenner has always been with the Yankees. His way, or no way. So Washington Heights and the Dominicans came downtown for Sosa, who had made them all feel uptown all summer long as he chased McGwire and McGwire sometimes chased him.

Around one o'clock, seven hours before the first pitch of the '98 World Series, Church Street—one block from Broadway—is jammed with traffic and the people are racing up the stairs from the subway station on Chambers Street, around the corner. You can get Duke Ellington's A train at Chambers Street, but today they were trying to catch a ride with Sosa, let him carry them along one more time, the way he and McGwire had carried baseball. There are young men in T-shirts and baggy jeans, holding the flags of the Dominican Republic, that flag flying proudly over baseball for one more afternoon, this one in New York. You heard horns and sirens and a happy, excited music that seemed to come up off the sidewalks and be more vowels than consonants.

There would be Dominicans who would boycott the day and the parade because they were still angry at Giuliani for taking it out of Washington Heights. But the crowds came out, anyway. There were so many kids. You saw fathers and sons, a lot of them, the children waving smaller flags.

You saw whole families: a snapshot of modern New York City here on the streetcorner on Saturday morning as fine and real as any shot of the skyline.

Osvaldo Martinez had come from Brooklyn. He was thirty-two. He was another who was mad at the mayor, but when asked why he had come, he said, "To see Sammy Sosa."

He smiled and said, "To say thank you in person to Sammy Sosa."

They sold Sosa T-shirts on the corners. Some of the flags now were three feet wide. The parade will end at City Hall Park, where all parades like this end, great or small. The park is beginning to fill up. The first game of the Series when the Series is in New York always feels like the best possible baseball holiday; if the day Sosa caught McGwire felt like a big holiday in Washington Heights, this was bigger now, at the other end of Manhattan. There seemed to be parents everywhere in the park, more small children, all here to see their hero. By 2:30, the mix of American flags and Dominican flags seems almost equal in City Hall Park. Couples dance the merengue.

And you begin to hear the chant:

Sosa.

Sosa.

Sosa.

The floats come out of lower Broadway, the sound of marching bands with them. Maybe there are 3,000 people in the park now, maybe more. Then they see Sosa under the tented bandstand, and the park explodes. As if he had just gone deep again. Everywhere, the kids are on their fathers' shoulders. Sosa, facing uptown, waves at them, smiles as if he can see all the way to Washington Heights.

Giuliani speaks and is booed, then cheered as he declares this Sammy Sosa Day in New York. Finally it is Sosa's turn. He begins in English, switches to Spanish, and by the end the words don't matter, it is just the sight of him, here in front of them, and now they are chanting not just his name, but this:

MVP.

MVP.

MVP.

"I will see you in Washington Heights tomorrow!" he yells in Spanish.

In the very back of the crowd, there is a father with his son, not much bigger than Zach, sitting on his shoulders.

In both English and Spanish, the father says, "You see him? You see him, *m'hijo?* You see Sammy? You see him?"

The boy nods his head, weaves back and forth to the music. Yes, he could see him. He would remember seeing Sammy Sosa in person like this his whole life. He would know that he saw Sosa the year Sosa hit 66.

I never saw Mantle in person in '61.

I never saw Maris.

If the boy in City Hall Park didn't know how lucky he was, his father would tell him.

IN GAME 1 OF THE '98 SERIES, THE PADRES AND Yankees gave Sosa a game he could understand perfectly, a game that fit the summer, and the season.

They gave Sosa, gave all of us, more home runs.

What else?

Greg Vaughn hit two for the Padres. Gwynn hit his home run so hard, it made you remember something Reggie Jackson had said after hitting one up there, back in October of '81. One memory always bouncing off another here, then another. It was Game 5 of a Divisional Series between the Yankees and Brewers, and Reggie killed one off a Milwaukee pitcher named Moose Haas, and afterward Jackson was asked where the ball landed after it went crashing off the facing of the upper deck in right.

"Second f—ing base," Jackson said.

So the Padres had three home runs and a 5–2 lead, and going into the bottom of the seventh, they were nine outs away from getting all they wanted out of their weekend trip to New York City: a split off the Yankees. If they got a split the way the Indians had gotten a split because of Chuck Knoblauch's play, then they'd take their chances when they got back to San Diego for Games 3, 4, and 5. "We've got nothing to lose," Gwynn had said. "Nobody except us expects us to win this thing."

But they were certainly winning Game 1.

Then came the end of the World Series for the Padres. They would lose this Series in the first game as surely as the A's had lost to the Dodgers because of Kirk Gibson's home run off Dennis Eckersley in 1988, as surely as the A's had lost to the Reds in '90 because of Eric Davis's home run off Dave Stewart. Maybe Stewart knew best of all in the Padres' dugout, where he now worked as pitching coach. Because you never forget. I had once asked Tim McCarver—working this game on television for Fox—how long it took him to get over the '68 Series. His magnificent Cardinals, trying to win its third World Series of the sixties, led the Tigers three games to one, and lost. McCarver put down a cigar, looked good and hard at me over his reading glasses as he prepared for a Mets game at Shea Stadium, said, "You never get over it." Stewart would never forget the pitch to Davis, where the ball landed in center field.

One pitch changing everything.

Memories bouncing off memories at the Series, in the Stadium.

This time it was one inning, in Game 1. There would be more Series after that. El Duque would win a World Series game, and Scott Brosius would hit a dramatic three-run homer in Game 3, and Mariano Rivera, who couldn't get those last outs against the Indians in the playoffs of '97, would get all the outs he needed in Game 4, when the Yankees finished off their sweep of the Padres.

The great moment of the Series, though, was the bottom of the seventh in Game 1, when the Yankees rolled a seven against the Padres. Kevin Brown was out of the game for the Padres and Donne Wall had replaced him, and now he was facing Knoblauch with two men on base. And this time Knoblauch lost the ball the way you are supposed to, the way everybody had been losing them in baseball all season. He lost it over the left-field wall. It took a long time to come down, the way the ball had taken a long time to come down in October of '78, when Bucky Dent had been the unlikely home-run hero for the Yankees, the day Dent struck Fenway dumb. No such problem now at Yankee Stadium, which sounded like some kind of baseball revival meeting, on the night when Knoblauch found official redemption for not chasing after the ball Tino Martinez had thrown him against the Indians.

It was 5–5 in Game 1, and the Yankees weren't done yet. Pretty soon they had the bases loaded and Mark Langston had replaced Wall, and he was facing Martinez. Left-handed pitcher against left-handed hitter. Knoblauch had wiped the books clean. Maybe Martinez could do the same. Maybe there was enough redemption to go around for everybody.

For three seasons, ever since he had replaced Don Mattingly at first base for the Yankees, Martinez had been one of the most popular and productive Yankees. He had been booed at the Stadium after taking over for Mattingly, but Martinez had hit his way past all that. This year, even after taking that fastball in the back from Armando Benitez of the Orioles, he had finished with 28 home runs and 123 RBIs. He had become only the fourth Yankee in history (the others being Ruth, Gehrig, and DiMaggio) to drive in more than 120 runs two seasons in a row.

The only problem was this: Martinez had done nothing for the Yankees in the postseason. When the Yankees had gone to Atlanta for the middle three games of the '96 World Series—and had to play without a designated hitter, because teams don't use them in the National League park during the Series—Joe Torre had benched the slumping Martinez in favor of Cecil Fielder. Martinez was 1-for-11 in that Series. As a Yankee, Martinez was just 18-for-96 in the postseason coming into Game 1 against the Padres, and then he was 0-for-2 against Brown. Already, because love can fade fast in New York, Martinez was reading and hearing that the Yankees might trade him during the winter and sign free agent Mo Vaughn to take his place at first base.

"Nobody has to tell me that I'm struggling," Martinez had said to me the day before, in front of his locker. "Believe me, I'm aware of that. But that's why I know I have such a tremendous opportunity now. I have a chance to make a difference in the World Series."

Martinez smiled. He is not the biggest talker on the team, but you could tell he had been thinking about this, about doing something— anything—and turning his October around.

"You can't help but think about making that one play," he said. "Making that one anything that wins the game for your team."

Mark Langston went to a 3–2 count on Martinez. Langston thought he had struck Martinez out at 2–2, but Rich Garcia, the home-plate umpire, said the pitch was low. So Martinez, who had been striking out all month in moments like this, even as the Yankees kept winning, was not struck out now. He still had the opportunity he had talked about the day before, he still had the chance to do something.

Langston threw, and Martinez hit one into the upper deck in right field.

Grand slam.

McGwire had settled the first game of the season, set the tone, with a grand slam in March. Now Martinez settled the first game of the World Series with a grand slam on the seventeenth of October.

At the end of Sammy Sosa Day in New York City.

I WATCHED THE LAST TWO GAMES OF THE WORLD Series on television. Taylor was in the last month of pregnancy by then, and there had been one brief scare about Hannah coming prematurely while I was in Cleveland for the Yankees–Indians series. My wife was too close, San Diego was too far.

So I watched the games with the boys until it was time for them to go to bed. Even in what seemed like the most perfect of seasons, the World Series games started too late in too much of the country, sent too many kids to bed before the good parts.

They were long gone by the time Brosius, the eventual MVP of the World Series, threw the ball across the diamond to Martinez for the last out. Before they would celebrate on the field. Before even a tough guy like George Steinbrenner would cry on national television during the presentation of the World Series trophy.

Before the Yankees would place a long-distance phone call to Darryl Strawberry in New Jersey, and talk to him one by one, handing the phone down the blue line, all the way home.

I wrote out three last notes, took them upstairs, placed them by the beds, one by one.

Chris had a big color photograph of El Duque on his wall, one

I hadn't noticed before. Alex had laid out his Sosa jersey to wear to school the next day. It was next to his glove; the weather was still good, they were still playing ball at recess at his school. Zach had the ball Darryl had signed for him on the nightstand next to his bed, along with one he'd gotten from David Cone. They slept peacefully, not knowing the Yankees had won, that they had gotten the ending they wanted.

Not knowing it was next season already.

Dear Zach:
Yankees win.
Th-uh-uh-uh Yankees win!
I love you forever.
Remember this season forever.
Love, Dad.

After the Season

TWO DAYS AFTER THE YANKEES FINISHED OFF THE Padres in Game 4, the morning of a Yankee parade in the Canyon of Heroes as big as any war hero or astronaut or ballplayer had ever seen, I waited for Darryl Strawberry in the parking lot across from Yankee Stadium. A month earlier, he had walked into this lot and gotten into his car before Game 2 of the Yankee–Ranger series and driven away from the season. Now he would come back to it, ride in the lead car of the parade, a red Cadillac convertible, with his wife Charisse.

His black Jeep finally made the turn at 157th Street and Ruppert Place about 9:30, with the blue-and-white Academy buses that would take the whole Yankee family downtown lined up outside the ballpark. Darryl would be on one of those buses. A baseball October that had begun with the quiet word "cancer" at the hospital would end with a sound in the Canyon of Heroes that maybe only baseball still makes.

"I wanted to hear the city today," he said when he got out of the car. "I wanted to see my teammates."

They had visited him in the hospital, called him after all the big wins on the way to the finish line. But another baseball thing that never ever changes: You are a ballplayer when you are at the ballpark. You are a Yankee at Yankee Stadium. When Strawberry got out of his car, Chili Davis was there to greet him.

"Welcome home," Davis said.

You remembered the T-shirt Davis had given out to Strawberry and the rest of the Yankees: Don't Send No Boys.

Not to this parade.

The surgery had been a success; the doctors had found a spread of the cancer to only one of thirty-six lymph nodes. Soon Strawberry would fly to his southern California home and begin a winter of chemotherapy, already talking about next season, already thinking about the spring. But first this parade. Strawberry spent some time with the Yankees in the clubhouse. When he came back up the stairs, stood under the portrait of the '27 Yankees on the outside, Joe Torre saw him.

"Hey, Skip," Darryl said. "How you doin'?"

"Even better now," Torre said, and hugged Strawberry and came out of that crying.

It would be a day of cheers, tears. Strawberry riding in the red Cadillac. El Duque Hernandez riding with his daughters, with whom he had just been reunited that morning. With the help of Vice President Al Gore, Attorney General Janet Reno, New York City's John Cardinal O'Connor, and George Steinbrenner, the two girls—Yahumara, eight, and Steffi, three—had been granted temporary visas out of Cuba by Fidel Castro. They had made the trip with Hernandez's mother, Maria Pedroso, and his ex-wife, Norma Manso.

"When it appeared Castro was prepared to make this happen, so that a guy's family could be with him at his moment of triumph," Leon Fuerth, Gore's national security adviser, said, "it was the right thing to do."

"Yo amo a Nueva York," Hernandez kept yelling from his float, from the microphone at City Hall Park later.

He loved New York.

The pictures in the papers the next day would show him at Teterboro Airport in New Jersey when the plane carrying his family arrived, when he saw his daughters for the first time since he had gotten into the boat the previous December. Hernandez had a glass of champagne in one hand, better than any he had tasted in San Diego, because he had Steffi, wearing a Yankee cap, in the other.

Fathers and daughters, one last time.

Maybe the best time.

WE TURNED THE PAGE IN NOVEMBER, AS WE ALWAYS do in baseball. Bernie Williams nearly left the Yankees for the Red Sox—a reverse Ruth—but, the day before Thanksgiving, signed an $87.5 million contract with the Yankees, a deal that could eventually be worth $100 million.

So Williams would stay in center field at the Stadium, keep his own grace out there, so there would be days and nights when we would continue to compare him to DiMaggio, who was still in the hospital in late November when he turned eighty-four.

There was the night when I called my father and told him that it wasn't pneumonia, that DiMaggio had been battling lung cancer. I gave him the news about Joe DiMaggio's cancer the way I had given my sons the news about Darryl's.

"He's sicker than they've been telling us, Pop," I said.

He said, "I thought it must be something worse when they announced right away that he wouldn't be out of the hospital for six weeks."

There was a pause, and then he said, "More cancer."

"Too much."

Another pause, and then my father said, "I'll say a prayer for him."

Sounding like Alex.

The off-season of '98 and '99 went on. Sosa was elected MVP in a landslide; the only first-place vote Mark McGwire got came out of St. Louis. Mo Vaughn left the Red Sox for the Angels. Albert Belle, who nearly came to the Yankees at that time when they thought they would lose Williams, left the White Sox for the Orioles. Randy Johnson signed for $52 million with the Arizona Diamondbacks and Kevin Brown got $105 million from the Dodgers and suddenly Roger Clemens was demanding a trade from the Blue Jays. The money was crazy, because it always is, and the division between rich and poor in baseball became more and more dramatic, more troubling. There was talk that Steinbrenner would sell his controlling interest in the Yankees to the giant Cablevision, which broadcasts Yankee games on the Madison Square Garden network, for more than $500 million.

After the perfect season, with headlines about home runs, almost always about triumph, we had an off-season of headlines about money and player movement.

So it is not a perfect game and never has been and never will be. The only perfect games come on those dream days when imperfect men like Larsen, like Wells, pitch like immortals. Those of us who love baseball truly will always worry about the people who run the game, because even in the best of times they seem to lack vision and perspective, sometimes the proper strength and character. They nearly killed baseball with shortsightedness in 1994, and they could do it again. Suddenly, Rupert Murdoch owns the Dodgers and owns Fox, which broadcasts so much baseball regionally and nationally, and even has fifty Yankee games on Fox's Channel 5 in New York. These are outrageous conflicts of interests, whether baseball is in a boom period or not. But nobody says anything. The game cries out for the kind of real revenue-sharing they have in the National Football League, because it is the only way for smaller markets to even the field with Murdoch, Steinbrenner, Turner, Disney. Nobody says very much about that, either. The Yankee payroll climbs toward $85 million at a time when the top offer for the entire Kansas City Royals franchise is $75 million.

A perfectly imperfect game.

McGwire's 70 home runs, Sosa's 66, those 125 games the Yankees won, none of that changes that baseball games can still run too long, that the umpires seem to make up a new strike zone from game to game, city to city, sometimes inning to inning. The umpires have become too arrogant, the agents too powerful. There will always be too much romance attached to it all, by me, by everybody else. Even at the end of a glorious season, the ratings for a four-game World Series are lower than expected.

But you do not measure baseball by ratings. It is not a big, slam-bang action sport for television, for Video Game America, and never will be. You measure baseball at the turnstiles, where from April through October every year, every season, the people come out to watch. And begin the conversation that never really seems to stop. About balls flying over walls, and bouncing off walls. Memories triggering other memories, in big, beautiful places. In what is still the most beautiful game we have.

It is something that is passed on. It is something you see all around you at the ballpark on a summer afternoon, when Piazza is at Shea Stadium, and hope is with him. I go to all the sports events with my children, all the time, and I would always rather take them to the ballpark, and they would rather be there than anywhere else. *I* hope that one of the reasons is because they are there with me. Someday soon I hope my daughter will join us. Just because our small corner of the ballpark always seems to feel like such a small safe bright corner of the world.

I cannot tell you for sure why baseball is passed on the way it is, more than the other sports. I just know it came first with me. It was something I shared with my father, and still share today. It was a special language that we had, at the ballpark, in the front seat of a '56 Dodge, watching on television. Talking on the telephone the night McGwire hit No. 62, all that time after we had watched Maris hit No. 61. A love that fits inside of a bigger love, like a ball in a mitt.

With its own sweet sound track, always.

There is a night in November, when I hear Alex come running out of the game-watching room, yelling, "Dad, Sosa hit another!"

I think he is watching some replay of the season. It turns out he is watching a game from Japan, a touring team of All-Stars from this country playing the Japanese All-Stars. And Sosa has indeed hit one out. The camera finds him in the dugout, mugging for that camera, blowing kisses to us all.

Later that night, putting Alex down, I stand in front of the shelves where he has now moved The Stuff. The balls on the top shelf. The plaque that includes his team picture from the Ontarios. The signed photographs on a lower shelf. But I can't find his McGwire card, the one from Roger Dean Stadium in the spring.

His special card for the home run season.

"Where's your McGwire?" I say.

"I traded it."

Very matter-of-fact.

"You traded your *McGwire?*" I ask. "Who'd you trade it to?"

"The man at the card store."

It still comes out *"cowd* store" with Alex. There is a part of me that hopes it always will.

"What did you get for it?"

He smiles brilliantly, lighting up the stars on his ceiling.

"Four Sosas," he says proudly.

For him then, it is still the summer of '98.

I watched it with my sons, and with my father. And found myself hoping that in another baseball summer someday, one way down the road when I was old and looking to feel young, when new heroes would chase the same old records and more home runs than you could ever believe would fill the sky, that my sons would still love baseball the way they do now. And that they would, in that distant summer, still love me the way I love my father.